DENIM

FROM COWBOYS TO CATWALKS
A VISUAL HISTORY OF THE WORLD'S MOST LEGENDARY FABRIC

GRAHAM MARSH AND PAUL TRYNKA   **FASHION EDITOR: JUNE MARSH**

AURUM PRESS

AN INDIGO PRODUCTION

Art Direction and Design: GRAHAM MARSH

Written by PAUL TRYNKA

Fashion Editor: JUNE MARSH

Photo Research: JANE TITTERINGTON

First published in Great Britain 2002 by Aurum Press Limited
25 Bedford Avenue, London WC1B 3AT

ISBN 1 85410 791 7
1   3   5   6   4   2
2002 2004 2006 2005 2003

Printed in Singapore by CS Graphics

ACKNOWLEDGEMENTS
Curtis Trynka, Glyn Callingham, Cavan Cooper, Tony Crawley, Geoff Dann, Trevor
Gray, The Crew from the Island, Max and Coco Katz, Warren Knight, Tony
Nourmand, Peter Rogers, Michael Stier, Dennis Alstrand, Keiji Amemiya, Paola
Brandi, Jean at Dispensary for kids, Sarah Edwards, Carl Glover & Christine
Bone, Adriano Goldschmied, Peter Ingwersen, Grumbler for bike information,
http://home.att.net/~grumbler, Peter Liebman, The MOJO Team, Nancy McLure,
Marly Nijssen, Jeff Pirtle, JC Penney, Terry Rawlings, Holly Stewart, Hannah
Tausz, Lucy Wise. Special thanks to Lynn Downey and Stefano Aldighieri of
LS&Co. for their expert assistance, inexhaustible patience and fact-checking of
the manuscript (any remaining errors are strictly the responsibility of the
authors); also to Joe Vega, who does a heroic job of maintaining the Lee archives.

Thanks for access to the vintage denim collection of:
Heller's Cafe Inc.
1654 East Olive Way
Seattle Washington 98102
Tel 206 322 7130
Fax 205 322 2794

JMARK,
P.O. Box 5178,
Santa Monica,
CA 90409
Tel 310 396 9767
All rights to JMARK images remain with JMARK

All trademarks acknowledged.
Levi's, 501 are registered trademarks of Levi Strauss & Co. 1155 Battery Street,
San Francisco. Lee and Wrangler are trademarks of VF Corporation.

Indigo productions: paultrynka@compuserve.com

INTRODUCTION

Presidents and prime ministers wear it. It's still a rebel fabric. A badge of workers, a totem of anti-establishment cool, denim is the most democratic of fabrics, one that flatters everyone but the powerful and paunchy.

The story of denim nestles snugly against the curves and sinews of American history: a look conceived by the French, a technology perfected by the English, a form of clothing invented by two Americans – one recently arrived from the Baltic, the other from Bavaria. Nurtured in an immigrant culture, it was worn by workers and popularized by American icons from John Wayne to Madonna. Unique among fabrics, it occupies four dimensions: the warp and the weft are clearly distinguished, likewise the front and back. Yet thanks to a molecular quirk of the indigo that colours it, denim moves in the dimension of time. A pair of well-worn jeans tells the story of its owner, a unique dialogue which is only matched by the finest of furniture, which gains a patina with age, or a Cremonese violin, whose cell structure and varnish are transmuted by the music played upon it. But denim is industrial, cheap and looks good when dirty. It gets old, like us, and then gets thrown away.

Denim is simple, non-intellectual stuff. But it abounds in dualities. It is a symbol of egalitarianism and of materialism; it embodies the freedom of the west and is traded in closed societies in lieu of hard currency. It ages gracefully, yet signifies an obsession with youth. It glories in its ubiquity, but it looks different on everyone who wears it.

On my way out of San Francisco, where I'd pored over a 120-year-old pair of Levi's and debated the lifestyle of their owner – his height, his work, what he kept in his pocket – I met a young Australian who was travelling around the States opening a string of juice bars. She could never wear jeans for a business meeting, she told me; it sent out the wrong message. Then she told me why we wrote this book.

"I love my jeans. They make me feel horny."

A RIVETING TALE
When Jacob met Levi – and created a legend

Jacob Davis had a difficult customer.

The woman lived close to his tiny tailor's shop in Reno, Nevada, and was in search of a pair of pants for her husband. A woodcutter apparently bloated with dropsy, he was too big for regular pants, and without pants he couldn't work. It was December 1870; she needed the pants by January, when he'd be out cutting wood again. And those pants needed to be strong – workmen's trousers wore out quickly.

Jacob was paid the $3 for the custom-made pants in advance. He soon set to crafting them using a sturdy white cotton duck fabric he'd purchased from a helpful dry goods supplier in San Francisco, named Levi Strauss.

Jacob had stitched the pants when his eyes alighted on a pile of rivets that he used for attaching straps to the horse blankets he supplied to a local blacksmith. "The rivets were lying on the table," he remembered a couple of years later. "The thought struck me to fasten the pockets with those rivets." He hammered the rivets into the corners of the pockets, reckoning they would help the woodcutter's pants hold out that bit longer. "I did not make a big thing of it. I sold those pants and never thought of it for a time."

In February Jacob sold around ten pairs of his riveted pants to local teamsters. In March he sold even more, his business spreading by word of mouth as his customers concluded they stood up to more wear and tear than anything they'd seen before. It was a much-needed break. An immigrant from Riga, on the Baltic, Davis had tried making a living as a brewer, a coal merchant and a tobacconist before moving to Reno in 1868; he'd even essayed a career as an inventor, applying for patents on a steam-powered canal boat and an ore-crusher. This new invention generated cash where its predecessors had failed because the riveted pants fetched a hefty premium over

Jacob Davis (top left) is the unsung hero of Levi's history. He came up with the idea of strengthening work overalls using copper rivets, enlisted the help of Levi Strauss (top centre) to secure a patent and oversaw production of early Levi's (top right, riveted back pocket of early cotton duck Levi's).

Right: a mysterious late 19th century studio portrait, labelled "Yuma Indian", of a Native American sporting Levi's 501 Waist Overalls. It now resides in the Levi Strauss & Co. Archives.

conventional overalls. All the same, the $68 dollars it would take to apply for another patent was a lot of money. This time round, Jacob Davis would spread the risk.

On 5 July 1872 Jacob sat down and wrote a letter to his fabric supplier. He explained to Levi Strauss that the riveted pants were so popular "that I cannot make them up fast enough. My nabors are getting yealouse of these success and unless I secure it by patent papers... everybody will make them up."

Offering a half share in his invention if Strauss funded the patent application, Jacob enclosed two examples of his new pants so that the San Francisco merchant could see this innovation for himself. One pair was in the white cotton duck. The other pair was blue, fashioned from denim supplied by Strauss. One of his most popular lines, the denim was made at the Amoskeag factory in New Hampshire.

Levi's reply to Jacob's letter has never surfaced – it was probably lost in the San Francisco earthquake and fire of 1906 – but his response was favourable and speedy. On 9 August Levi's lawyers filed the joint patent application for an "improvement in fastening seams". The patent was finally granted in May 1873, by which time Jacob had

Levi Strauss & Co. was already a thriving concern before the company produced its first Waist Overalls. Here the sales force poses in front of the Battery Street building that LS&Co. occupied from 1866. The building burned to the ground in the 1906 San Francisco earthquake.

8

These cotton duck overalls are probably the closest surviving relatives of the very first pair of riveted Waist Overalls crafted by Jacob Davis in January 1871. Before denim became the more popular finish, Levi Strauss & Co. also made overalls in cotton duck; this was probably the cause of the erroneous notion that Levi's first "denim" jeans were made of sailcloth dyed blue. These Youth's Waist Overalls date from around 1880 and, like all early Levi's, feature just one back pocket, with the early, non-Two Horse Brand label, in this case placed centrally. Denim always seemed to have been the more popular option; LS&Co. stopped making cotton duck overalls in 1911. Below, left: the May 1873 patent for Jacob Davis's "Improvement In Fastening Pocket-Openings" – the document which launched a billion jeans!

The earliest-known pair of Levi's jeans. These were acquired by Levi Strauss & Co. for $45,000 in an Ebay auction in May 2001. Dating from the 1880s, they predate the 501; the shape is different, with more of a "work-pant" cut similar to that of the Youth's Waist Overalls on page 9. The widely-spaced seam stitching on the single back pocket is characteristic of Levi's workwear, as opposed to the 501, while the "pliers pocket" is also rarely seen on Levi's jeans. Note the all-white selvage edge of the Amoskeag denim, which has a greener cast than later, Cone denim – perhaps because Amoskeag used natural vegetable (as opposed to synthetic) indigo dye. The copper rivets, stamped "Pat May 1872, LS&Co SF" are also unique to early Levi's Waist Overalls.

moved to San Francisco to oversee clothes production for Levi's new business.

Why did Jacob fix on Levi Strauss as a potential business partner? Perhaps it was simply the fact that Strauss had been a helpful supplier who extended him credit. Perhaps it was the common bond of their Jewish faith. Perhaps it was simply Levi Strauss's reputation as an honest businessman, a reputation that would later be reinforced with acts of largesse and philanthropy, and one that Jacob knew about, for in his first letter to Levi he enclosed a $350 check, which left him a large credit balance, telling Levi "The reason I send so much money is because I have no use for it, and you may alowe me interest as well as the bank." Whatever the reason, it was a fateful choice.

Loeb Strauss was born in Bavaria in 1829, and followed his brothers Louis and Jonas to New York in 1847; he anglicized his name to Levy, then Levi, around 1850. In 1853

Although Levi Strauss (shown sitting far left) never married, he was the head of an extended family. Levi's sister, Fanny Stern, was widowed around 1874; her sons Jacob, Louis, Abraham and Sigmund Stern would take over the company following Levi's death.

he moved to San Francisco and founded Levi Strauss & Co. – in effect, the West Coast branch of the Strauss family business. However grandiose the firm's title, Levi's early career must have been essentially that of a travelling salesman. Over the next twenty years, however, he built the company into a thriving wholesale business, selling fabrics, clothing and boots from its headquarters at 14–16 Battery Street.

Levi had only sold clothes made by other people; actually making the product was an entirely new enterprise. Davis organized the production process, probably initially by sending pre-cut stacks of fabrics, buttons and rivets to seamstresses around the city. Many of those early pants were made from brown cotton duck (which would later give rise to the erroneous assumption that Levi's first "jeans" were made from brown canvas dyed blue). But as word spread of Levi's sturdy new riveted pants, demand grew for the blue version, made in the denim his company bought from Amoskeag. Nobody knows

Jacob or Sigmund Stern, relaxing with pooch, San Francisco. The Sterns took over LS&Co. in 1902; by 1919, thanks to a drop in cotton prices, the company's future looked grim.

BLUE EYES
MINE

HE LAST CHANCE MINE

exactly when, but by 1925 Levi Strauss & Co.'s customers started referring to them using a new term: jeans.

From the vantage point of the twenty-first century, it's easy to define Jacob and Levi's riveted denim pants as the first pair of jeans. Yet behind that indisputable fact lie many tangled threads. The first is the origin of denim itself. The name is generally thought to derive from "Serge De Nimes", a twill fabric made in the textile-producing town in the south of France. More recently it's been suggested that the name comes from another fabric called simply "nim". In any case, both these French fabrics were made from a wool and silk mix, whereas the denim produced in America from the late eighteenth century was made from cotton. Quite possibly the missing link came from textile mills in Lancashire, England, which by 1800 were producing a fabric named denim, made out of cotton and probably designed to echo the look of French wool/silk twills. There was also another, entirely different fabric made in the States called jean, which derived from woollen fabric woven in Genoa, Italy. It was used to make cheap pants, but as true "jean" fabric fell out of favour, the name seemed to transfer to denim pants.

By 1800 the USA boasted a booming textiles industry. The Amoskeag Manufacturing Company in New Hampshire was one of the biggest producers; opened in 1804, it introduced its first denim in the middle of the century. A twill fabric that used one coloured and one plain thread, it bore only a slight resemblance to its French or English predecessors, which were generally piece-dyed. Significantly, the coloured thread was almost invariably dyed with indigo; a chemical quirk means that indigo's molecules simply sit on the surface of the cotton thread it dyes. As the fabric is worn, the indigo chips off. Denim wears itself in. It was the perfect medium for Levi's new product.

Apart from the rivets, Levi's trousers were not significantly different from those of his competitors. But Levi Strauss concentrated on pants, or Waist Overalls, as opposed to

Levi Strauss was a pioneer of what today we'd call "brand identity", as shown by the oilcloth guarantee label, introduced in 1892 (this early example, which proclaims "This is a pair of them", rather than "This is a pair of Levi's", dates from circa 1908), and the Two Horse Brand patch, shown here on a pair of 201 jeans – which, being the budget line, bore a linen rather than a leather patch.

Levi's pants were popular with miners – the photo opposite captures two Levi's wearers at the Blue Eyes Mine. To this day turn of the century examples are discovered in abandoned mine shafts. If they're genuine Levi's, they could be worth tens of thousands of dollars; rival brands, unfortunately for many would-be denim gold-diggers, are generally worth only several hundreds of dollars...

Levi Strauss & Co. always produced an extensive range of clothing in addition to its blue jeans. These baby denim overalls date from around 1905, the cord pants from around 1919.

Denim, as we understand the term today, was in its early days unique to American mills. Levi's fabric was first produced by New Hampshire's huge Amoskeag factory complex (below). In 1915, LS&Co. started to use denim from North Carolina's Cone Mills (main picture, left), which is still one of the world's biggest suppliers.

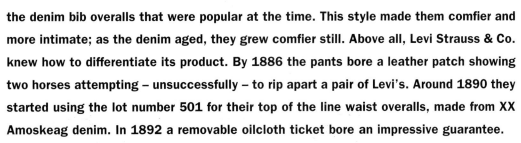

the denim bib overalls that were popular at the time. This style made them comfier and more intimate; as the denim aged, they grew comfier still. Above all, Levi Strauss & Co. knew how to differentiate its product. By 1886 the pants bore a leather patch showing two horses attempting – unsuccessfully – to rip apart a pair of Levi's. Around 1890 they started using the lot number 501 for their top of the line waist overalls, made from XX Amoskeag denim. In 1892 a removable oilcloth ticket bore an impressive guarantee.

Jacob Davis had supplied the simple technical innovation that differentiated Levi's product. But it was Levi's vision that effected a subtle transubstantiation, as these simple pants, originating from a cottage industry in Reno, Nevada, became an international phenomenon. Levi had started with a good product. He emphasized and consistently advertised its superiority. By 1900 he was claiming the product was "known the world over". It would take fifty years, but Levi's lofty claim would be proved right.

Left: Bell bottoms weren't a 1960s invention; they were one of Levi Strauss's earliest lines. Made from luxury blue and gold denim manufactured by Amoskeag, these Spring Bottom Pants (below and left) feature ornate pocket design details and complex body-hugging tailoring. As the cigar-toting dandy on the cover of the 1905 catalogue proclaims, they were something of a luxury item.

Right: Although best-known for its jeans or Waist Overalls, LS&Co. also produced bib overalls and Koveralls – one-piece overalls for kids, invented by Simon Davis, Jacob's son. They are being produced here at an on-site factory set up at San Francisco's Panama Pacific International Exposition, 1915.

Although they'd later become synonymous with cowboys, Levi's 501 jeans first found favour in the mining and logging communities, as this Dorothea Lange photo of loggers in Ola, Idaho, 1939, demonstrates.

Opposite: The "Calico Mine" 501s were discovered in 1948 in the Calico Silver Mine in California's Mojave desert. Dating from around 1890, they're the oldest 501 jeans that still survive. The woman who found them patched them up and wore them for a while before writing to Levi Strauss & Co. The company bought them for $25 plus a few pairs of new jeans. The design details of cinch, or "buckle back", single pocket and suspender buttons remained until 1901, when the 501 gained a second back pocket to become the "five pocket" version. Inset: Vintage 501 details.

COPPER RIVETED CLOTHING

All Made in our Own Factory Where Only Women and Girl Operators are Employed.
Please order all goods by lot number. (List of sizes on page 4)

We have listed here the famous Levi Strauss & Co. (Two-Horse Brand) Copper Riveted Clothing. The best selling merchandise of their kind in the world.

Made from the best materials—cut full.

We invite particular attention to our new Amoskeag Gold Medal numbers; light weight, indigo dyed, strong and durable.

We are also listing our Boys' and Youths' Bib Overalls.

On all engineers' as well as on our boys' and youths' bib Overalls we are now using the "metal-elastic" suspenders, of which we have the exclusive right for the Pacific Coast. An illustration appears on the opposite page.

the "two horse" brand
NO. 2
9 Oz. Blue Denim

No.		Per doz.
201.	Overalls, 2 hip pockets	$8 75
202.	Overalls, 2 hip pockets, extra sizes	10 00
203.	Overalls, youths'	7 50
204.	Overalls, boys'	6 50
209.	Overalls, Engineers', 7 pockets, new patent elastic suspenders	11 75
210.	Overalls, Engineers', 7 pockets, new patent elastic suspenders, extra sizes	13 00
211.	Jumpers, closed front	8 75
211E.	Jumpers, closed front, extra sizes	10 00
212.	Jumpers, open front	8 75
212E.	Jumpers, open front, extra sizes	10 00
213.	Blouses, pleated front	8 75
213E.	Blouses, pleated front, extra sizes	10 00
216.	Sack Coats, 4-piece, 5 pockets, large collar	11 75
216E.	Sack Coats, 4-piece, 5 pockets, large collar, extra sizes	13 00

8 Oz. Black Denim

No.		Per doz
224.	Coats, 5 pockets, 4-piece, large collars	$11 75
224E.	Coats, 5 pockets, 4-piece, large collars, extra sizes	13 00
225.	Overalls, 2 hip pockets	9 00
226.	Overalls, 2 hip pockets, extra sizes	10 25
221.	Overalls, Engineers', 7 pockets, patent elastic straps	11 75
222.	Overalls, Engineers', 7 pockets, patent elastic straps, extra sizes	13 00

XX
9 Oz. Amoskeag Blue Denim
Linen Sewed
For 30 Years the Standard

No.		Per doz.
501.	Overalls, 2 hip pockets	$10 50
502.	Overalls, 2 hip pockets, extra sizes	11 75
503.	Overalls, youths'	9 50
504.	Jumpers, closed front	10 50
504E.	Jumpers, closed front, extra sizes	11 75
505.	Jumpers, open front	10 50
505E.	Jumpers, open front, extra sizes	11 75
506.	Blouses, pleated front	10 50
506E.	Blouses, pleated front, extra sizes	11 75

9 Oz. Blue and Gold Mixed Denim

No.		Per doz.
511.	Spring Bottom Pants, 2 hip pockets	$15 00
512.	Spring Bottom Pants, 2 hip pockets, extra sizes	16 25
514.	Sack Coats, 4 pockets	14 50
515.	Vests	8 25

G. M.
Amoskeag Gold Medal Denim
Light Weight—Durable—Indigo Dyed.

No.		Per doz.
260.	Overalls, Engineers', 7 pockets, metal back suspenders	$11 75
261.	Overalls, Engineers', 7 pockets, metal back suspenders, extra sizes	13 00
264.	Sack Coats, 4-piece, 5 pockets, large collar	11 75
264E.	Sack Coats, 4-piece, 5 pockets, large collar, extra sizes	13 00

BOYS' AND YOUTHS' BIB OVERALLS
New Patent Elastic Suspenders.
Mode Duck Light Weight

No.		Per doz.
290.	Boys' 4 pockets	$6 00
291.	Youths' 4 pockets	7 25

Blue Light Weight

280.	Boys' 4 pockets	$6 50
281.	Youths' 4 pockets	7 75

RIVETED GOODS—Net 60 days, no discount for cash

REBATE TERMS
2½ per cent—Lots 200 and upwards will be subject to 2½ per cent rebate if fifty dozen or more have been used in six months—January 1st to July 1st, or July 1st to January 1st.

5 per cent—Lots 500 and upwards will be subject to 5 per cent rebate if twenty-five dozen or more have been used in six months as above. **Rebates Payable Semi-Annually.**

Prices subject to change without notice.

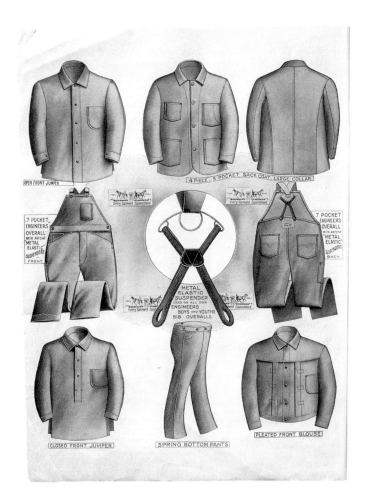

OPEN FRONT JUMPER

4 PIECE, 5 POCKET SACK COAT, LARGE COLLAR

7 POCKET ENGINEERS OVERALL WITH PATENT METAL ELASTIC SUSPENDERS FRONT

7 POCKET ENGINEERS OVERALL WITH PATENT METAL ELASTIC SUSPENDERS BACK

METAL ELASTIC SUSPENDER USED ON ALL OUR ENGINEERS BOYS AND YOUTHS BIB OVERALLS

CLOSED FRONT JUMPER

SPRING BOTTOM PANTS

PLEATED FRONT BLOUSE

The 201 Waist Overalls were a budget version of the 501; this pair dates from 1893, and unusually can be dated definitively because the unfortunate owner was wearing them when killed in a coaching accident. The 201 featured simpler stitching, in cotton rather than linen, and whereas the 501 was made of "9oz XX Amoskeag denim", that of the 201 remained unspecified, although of similar weight.

Opposite: The Levi's jacket – then termed "blouse" – appears in the 1905 catalogue, although it was probably introduced decades before. This 213, from 1910, is the budget version, with oilcloth label, unspecified denim and no pocket flap. The 506 was the full-price version, linen-sewn, using Amoskeag XX denim. The 1908 price list shows the comparative prices of the two ranges: $10.50 wholesale per dozen for either the 501 or 506, $8.75 per dozen for the 201 and 213.

HERMAN HEYNEMANN
Founder of Eloesser-Heynemann Co. Which for 96 Years Has Served the Pacific Coast....

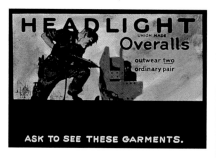

LET'S GO TO WORK
Overalls, workwear and two-dog labels

Around the 1990s, workwear became fashionable. Around the 1890s, workwear was obligatory. Although Levi's Waist Overalls would later become a global icon, before World War II the company's business was restricted to the West Coast; a variety of companies would establish the popularity of denim across the nation. In almost every case, their most popular products were bib overalls for the working man.

Early denim production was small-scale, but there were already many established manufacturers by the time Levi Strauss & Co. started making jeans in 1873. One major competitor was right on Levi's doorstep, at 33–55 Battery Street, San Francisco. Herman Heynemann opened for business in 1851, and was probably manufacturing denim clothing a decade or so before Levi Strauss. Heynemann's clothing bore the Can't Bust 'Em brand, and although most of the company's documentation, like that of Levi's, was destroyed in the San Francisco earthquake of 1906, the price list for that year boasts sixty-eight sizes of waist overalls, which were made in blue and black 9oz denim. Except for the rivets, Can't Bust 'Em's Model A Waist Overalls looked very similar to early Levi's pants. By the 1920s the Eloesser-Heynemann company had set up a string of dealers across San Francisco, Los Angeles and Portland, Oregon. Significantly, by 1925 Eloesser-Heynemann was referring to its black Waist Overalls as "Frisko Jeens", in recognition of what customers were actually calling the product, a move Levi's wouldn't make for another three decades.

Practically every geographical area boasted its own denim workwear manufacturer: Hamilton Carhartt set up his eponymous company in Detroit, 1884. OshKosh B'Gosh

Several companies predated LS&Co, as manufacturers of workwear, most notably Heynemann & Company, manufacturers of Can't Bust 'Em, who opened down the street from Levi Strauss in 1851. Washington Dee Cee, Carhartt and Headlight were all active in the workwear market by 1900; JC Penney started making its own workwear after a dispute with Levi Strauss & Co. in 1911.

Dorothea Lange captured for ever the face of Depression-era America with a series of haunting shots taken in the 1930s. This photo, taken in February 1936, is of One Eye Charlie, a labour contractor in the pea fields of San Luis Obispo County, California. Charlie's jeans look like Levi's, but are made by a rival company, probably Can't Bust 'Em; the rivet design differs slightly from Levi's.

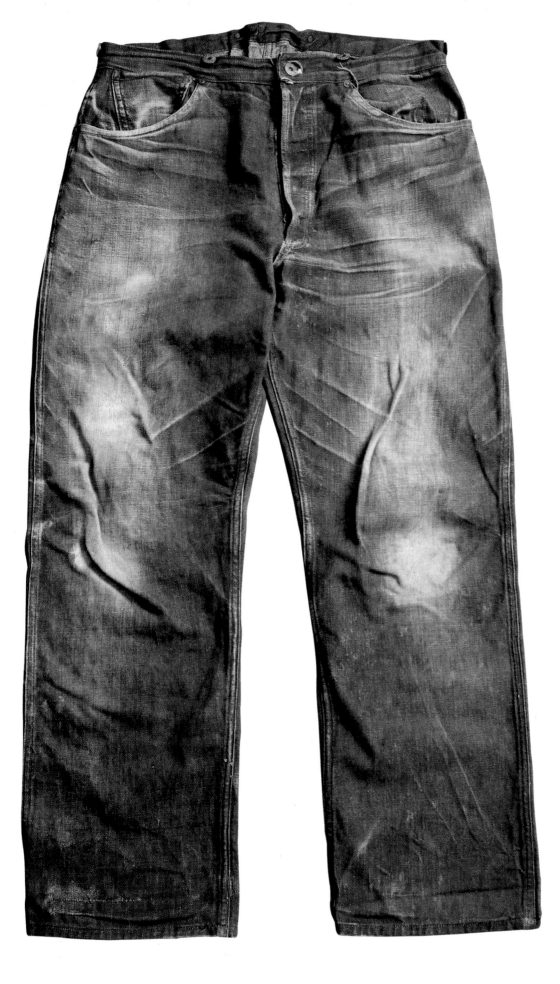

Around 1900, the Waist Overall market was a competitive one. California's Boss of the Road brand (main picture, left) was a major rival to Levi's. This cinchback pair, with suspender buttons and no belt loops, bears a strong resemblance to the Levi's 501 of circa 1920. Below, from top picture: back of the 1920s Boss of the Road; earlier, single-pocket Boss of the Road, with Levi's-style arcuate, from the turn of the century; Special jeans, again with Levi's-style arcuate; Stronghold jeans, made in Los Angeles and probably the leading brand in that area at the time. (Early Boss of the Road and Special courtesy Heller's Café; Stronghold courtesy JMARK).

"Something to Crow About"

ESTABLISHED 1851

CAN'T BUST 'EM Bib Overalls

UNION MADE

CAN'T BUST 'EM bib overalls are made in two general styles as illustrated.

EVERY FABRIC used in the construction of these garments is selected by the executive head of the firm. He chooses with the utmost care only such materials as are worthy of the Can't Bust 'Em trade mark.

EVERY SEAM THAT BEARS STRAIN is double sewed by a patented double-lock stitching machine—with the very toughest of thread. This strength permits us to say "Every stitch guaranteed."

EVERY POINT OF STRAIN and every pocket corner is reinforced by a *giant bar tack*. This reinforcement, without exception, is the strongest method known for the joining of two pieces of cloth. The ingenious machine which produces it puts stitch after stitch into the cloth, first in one direction and then across until the joint is unbreakable. By this process the threads of the cloth are not cut (as by the old fashioned copper rivet) and the giant bar tack gains strength as its threads shrink into the cloth after washing.

EVERY BUCKLE is the celebrated buckle described in detail on page 8.

EVERY BUTTON is built of solid metal—and wire stitched into the cloth, by a patented process which does not cut a single thread. This point in itself makes Can't Bust 'Ems easy to sell.

"Stitch after Stitch——the Giant Bar Tack"

The Eloesser-Heynemann showroom on Battery Street, San Francisco, circa 1905, and the company's Can't Bust 'Em factory, probably on Octavia and McAllister, circa 1915. The 1919 brochure shows details of Can't Bust 'Em's Model A Waist Overall; it featured bar-tacking on the back pocket, rather than "old fashioned copper rivets".

27

The H.D. Lee Mercantile Company started manufacturing workwear in 1911, but it was the invention of the Union-All – "shirt and pants all in one", and the ancestor of today's all-in-one overall – that put the company on the map. The Union-Alls pictured date from 1946. Above: the Union-Alls were endorsed by Babe Ruth.

Right: Lee marketed its product heavily; the company claims to have taken out the first national ad campaign for workwear in the US, in the Saturday Evening Post. This is the first of the series, from 1917.

At Last! A Nation's Need is Supplied-

DISCARD your old fashioned overalls, men! Slip on a suit of **Lee Union-Alls!** You'll never wear anything else to work in. Such an improvement! Such convenience! Such service! It's the work garment men in all walks of life have been waiting for. The mechanic, the motorist, the farmer, the laborer, the man who does odd jobs about the home and works in his garden—to every one of these, **Lee Union-Alls** are a revelation of comfort, convenience and serviceability. You'll forget there was ever such a word as "overall." Work clothing will mean **Union-Alls** to you first, last and all the time. Cost no more, either, than old fashioned, inconvenient, binding two-piece garments.

Lee Union-Alls are all in one piece (like your union underwear), which means there is no belt to bind, no double thickness at the waist, no jacket tails to get in the way. The suit slips on easily and quickly and can be worn conveniently and comfortably over clothing or next to your underwear. It is already the fastest selling work garment ever manufactured. You'll know why the minute you put on a suit.

Lee Union-Alls are made to endure the hardest wear—every strain point reinforced—all seams triple stitched; every button hole machine stitched; eight convenient pockets. **Lee Union-Alls** are made of Khaki, blue denim, express stripe, pin check or white drill.

Lee Union-Alls for children are made "just like Dad's," a complete one-piece suit, that pays its cost many times in the saving of clothing, washing bills, stockings, etc.

Lee Union-Alls are at first class dealers' everywhere. If your dealer cannot supply you, send your order direct to any of our factories, enclosing post office money order and stating size and material desired. Sent prepaid to any address in the U. S. Take no substitute. There is none "just as good."

MEN'S:
34 to 50 chest, $3.00
YOUTHS':
12 to 17 years,
$2.25

BOYS':
7 to 11 years
$1.75
CHILD'S:
2 to 6 years, $1.50

UNION Lee MADE Union-Alls
TRADE MARK REG.

DEALERS: If you wish to know more about this popular garment and the tremendous sales being made, write today.

The H. D. Lee Mercantile Co.
FACTORIES AND BRANCHES AT
Kansas City, Mo., Kansas City, Kans., Salina, Kans.
Waterbury, Conn., South Bend, Ind.

overalls were made in Oshkosh, Wisconsin from 1895. The Neustadter Brothers had launched the popular Boss of the Road jeans in Northern California before 1900. Hudson Overall Co., later to be known as Blue Bell, creators of Wrangler, opened for business in Greensboro, North Carolina in 1904. Stronghold brand jeans, which bore a strong resemblance to Levi's, were produced by Brownstein, Newmark and Louis in Los Angeles from the early 1900s. As denim workwear became more popular, heavyweights like Montgomery Ward, Chicago's Sears, Roebuck and Co., and JC Penney introduced their own lines, selling nationwide by around 1905–10. These bigger retailers usually had their workwear manufactured to their specifications by suppliers around the country: Sears, Roebuck and Co.'s Hercules brand, for instance, evolved over the years

Henry David Lee made his fortune in the oil business, selling out after an attack of pulmonary tuberculosis. He subsequently made another fortune with his grocery and clothing business. Here he poses, in pale suit, with his Union-Alls sales team.

Lee's Jelt denim overalls first appeared in 1925; Jelt denim used a tight weave and twisted yarn for extra strength. It proved a great success for Lee, not least because other workwear manufacturers used what was in effect the same fabric, Cone 818, but couldn't use the name that Lee had made famous with its consistent advertising.

Henry Lee was soon to become one of the biggest names in American workwear. Ironically, he'd opened his first factory in Kansas, still the home of Lee jeans today, because it was handy for the healing spa of Excelsior Springs.

Lee's Model 91 denim overalls were launched in 1926, gained the "Four In One" pocket in 1929, and became the company's flagship product, remaining in production for 50 years. This example dates from circa 1950. The Model 31 Overall (below) was a budget design, launched in 1931. This example dates from the 1930s.

Right: Lee was one of the first workwear manufacturers to use the zipper – which was then a proprietary name; Lee termed its own version a Whizit. The Whizit was fitted to both Union-Alls and bib overalls in 1928 and was apparently an instant success; in these photos taken after the 1930 National Corn Huskers Contest, eight of the ten winners are wearing Lee Whizits.

National Cornhusking Contest
8 of the First 10 Winners Wear the Famous Lee Whizits

Orville Chase—Wetmore, Kans.—Champion of Kansas—8th in national contest.

Valerius Altermatt—2nd in Minnesota—7th in national contest.

George Dickinson—Steamboat Rock, Iowa 2nd in Iowa—5th in national contest.

Bert Hanson—Mankato, Minn.—Champion of Minnesota—2nd in national contest.

Joe Korte—Petersburg, Neb.—2nd in Nebraska—6th in national contest.

Harold Holmes—Woodhull, Ill.—Champion of Illinois—4th in national contest.

Houston Franks—Erie, Illinois—2nd in Illinois—10th in national contest.

Charles Budd—Mishawaka, Ind.—Champion of Indiana—9th in national contest.

into stylish cowboy pants. JC Penney had retailed "Strauss overalls" at his Golden Rule stores as early as 1910. However, rival retailers complained that Penney was undercutting them with a retail price of just 58 cents. Levi's discontinued their supplies, and JC Penney introduced his own range; the Big Mac brand, for instance, was made by the Globe Corporation, in Abingdon, Illinois.

In many cases, would-be rivals opted for an unashamed rip-off of an existing brand (Indiana's Harrison and H company was advertising a "registered trade mark" of two *dogs* attempting to rip apart a pair of jeans in 1887, just one year after Levi Strauss & Co. introduced its two horse brand). In other cases, the products were unbranded and generic, assembled by small contractors using denim that early on came from the huge

Lee's workwear designs were often specifically designed for one type of worker. This Loco Jacket appeared in price lists in 1923; this example dates from 1949.

Amoskeag plant and was later sourced from North Carolina's denim mills, such as Edwin Mills or Cone. For many dealers and customers, the weight and source of the denim was more important than the actual maker; even today, it is easy to find vintage jeans that bear no maker's mark yet advertise they're made from "Cone Denim".

Most of the companies that are now bygone names lacked a simple USP that would differentiate their product from the competition, and hence perished in various economic downturns. But a company that invented a genuinely new product could prosper overnight. Such was the case with the H.D. Lee Mercantile Company, set up by Henry David Lee. Lee had made a fortune in the oil business before selling out to John Rockefeller's Standard Oil after a life-threatening attack of pulmonary tuberculosis.

The original caption on this photo reads: "Negroes gambling cotton money, outside Clarksdale, Mississippi, November 1939." (Note the improvised cardboard lampshade.) The photo illustrates why denim was avoided by urban African Americans in the 1950s and 1960s; it was indelibly linked with sharecropping and the impoverished South.

Against the advice of his doctors, and his lawyers, Lee set up a new company in 1889, believing Kansas and the Midwest were about to undergo an economic boom. The sales of groceries (including Lee Wonder Peas, Lee Fruit Salad Cocktail and Lee Black Raspberry Jelly), farming supplies and clothing proved him right, and in 1911 the Lee company started to make its own Waist Overalls and blouses in a second-storey factory over a motor car workshop in Salina, Kansas. Just two years later, in 1913, Henry Lee hit upon his own unique product: the Lee Union-All.

According to legend, the Lee Union-All was invented by Henry Lee's chauffeur, John Hemsley – despite the only evidence being the substantial sum of $5,000 Lee left to Hemsley in his will. In all probability it was a car mechanic from Detroit who wrote to Lee with the suggestion of replacing separate waist overalls and blouses with a one-piece garment. The H.D. Lee Mercantile Co. acted on his proposal, manufacturing the Lee Union-All in 1913, and consequently scoring a major coup with the Union-All's adoption by the US army in 1917. (The overalls' name reflected the fact that Lee's employees belonged to the United Garment Workers Of America; the Union-made tag on Lee and other products was as much a contemporary badge of political correctness as a designation of origin!) Lee advertised more heavily than its competitors, launching the Union-Alls with a national campaign via the Saturday Evening Post, and soon became one of the largest workwear manufacturers in the US, opening plants in Kansas City, Indiana, New Jersey and Minnesota, as well as a distribution outlet in California. Lee's

Levi Strauss & Co. produced bib overalls – or Engineers Overalls, as they termed them – under their Two Horse Brand, initially as the 205. They would never achieve the popularity of the company's Waist Overalls. This example dates from the 1920s. The company's Koveralls, despite their obvious debt to Lee's Union-Alls, were popular on the West Coast, and were retailed by JC Penney until a dispute over pricing.

Opposite: Skyscraper workers enjoy their lunch; denim bib overalls remained popular workwear until the 1980s – and more recently have become desirable fashion items, perhaps because of high-profile endorsement by rap artist Eminem.

The Harter Candy Co.
Mfg.....Confectioners
"The Home of Sweetheart Chocolates"

marketing wasn't all hard-sell; one of the company's most successful salesmen, Chester Reynolds, came up with the idea of a small doll wearing Lee overalls for use in shop window displays. Buddy Lee was an overnight success. Soon customers could buy their own for $1.25 including postage, his wardrobe extending to dozens of different outfits, including promotional regalia for Coca-Cola and Pepsi. Even today, pirate versions of Buddy are being sold by Japanese vintage denim dealers.

Lee's success in the workwear field continued with the launch of overalls made in Cone's new Jelt fabric in 1925. Made from very tightly twisted yarns, this 11 $\frac{1}{2}$ oz fabric was, it was claimed, as hard-wearing as conventional 13oz fabric. Later ad campaigns showed Jelt overalls being run over by steamrollers or stomped over by hundreds of heavy-footed pedestrians, without sustaining significant damage. The working man – and woman – seemed convinced. Although contemporary sales figures are not in existence, a 1940 survey by Dell Detective group's magazines of their readers concluded that Lee was the most popular overalls supplier, with 32% of the total market, followed by JC Penney's Pay-Day with 6.8% and Montgomery Ward with 5.6%. Lee's nascent rival on the West Coast didn't even get a mention.

Lee supplied company overalls to many major corporations, including Coca-Cola, Pepsi, Phillips 66 and Ford. These women are employees of the slightly less monumental Harter Candy Company; they were photographed circa 1917.

Diminutive denim icon Buddy Lee made his debut in 1920. He caused a major scare in 1951, when a flood wiped out Lee's Kansas City Distribution Center. A helicopter news team spotted rescue boats full of Lee employees attempting to save "babies" drowning in the street. Lee's entire stock was ruined – bar the Buddy Lee dolls, which floated.
From top left, Buddy appears in the guise of Play Suit, Loco, Athlete, Railroad, Cowboy, Specialty Uniform (Coca-Cola), Farmer, Industrial, Engineer, Tradesman, Engineer, Tradesman.

Although their market was confined to the West Coast in the 1920s and 1930s, Levi's jeans – or Waist Overalls, as the company still termed them – were omnipresent, thanks to the influence of Hollywood. Right: John Wayne poses for a still from Stagecoach, the epochal 1939 Western, wearing a classic pair of Levi's 501, with both belt loops and suspender buttons. Left: Country icon Roy Rogers and family demonstrate that Levi's were cool for kids, too.

HOME ON THE RANGE
The denim industry and the American cowboy

When the blues and country singers of the 1920s sang about not missing their water 'til their well ran dry, they were probably talking about love and sex. But there was another kind of loss in the air: the inescapable passing of Wild America. Thousands of cowboys were still running steers from the plains to the market, and riders on the Pony Express, long rendered obsolete by the telegraph, were still celebrities. Yet the new media of Hollywood – fortuitously located right on Levi's doorstep – and radio were already celebrating the American icon with an elegiac air. The cowboy was passing from real life into legend.

America's first country music station opened in 1919; others soon followed around the country, even as far as Mexico, which became the base for high-powered stations

Singer Bing Crosby, later regarded as a mere crooner, was at the cutting edge of the Los Angeles music scene in the 1930s. Here he poses with pipe and complete Levi's outfit of 501 jeans and 506 jacket. Bing's support of Levi's extended to the 1950s, when he was refused entrance to a hotel because he was wearing denim. Levi Strauss & Co. promptly made him a custom denim tuxedo, left, to prevent the problem recurring.

Opposite: The H.D. Lee Mercantile Company marketed itself heavily to the cowboy market in the Midwest; the cowboy shown in this ad from Dude Rancher Magazine, 1941, wears a pair of Lee 101 cowboy pants which, apart from the label, look rather similar to a pair of Levi's.

broadcasting right across the continent. As Sonny Payne of Arkansas station KFFA remembers, "Businesses such as JC Penney would always have a radio going – it drew crowds! The reaction was fabulous." The music that benefited most from this technological explosion was country – or "hillbilly". New musical dynasties like the Carter family sprang up overnight, soon to be followed by Western Swing bands like Bob Wills and His Texas Playboys and Gene Autry. All of them helped build a new cowboy mythology.

Over the same period the cowboy was becoming a mainstay of the burgeoning cinema industry. The first cowboy movie was 1904's The Great Train Robbery; just ten minutes in length, it was filmed by Edison Corporation technician and prototype auteur Edwin S. Porter. By 1914 the first feature-length Western movies were being made in Hollywood. Meanwhile, Levi's was directing its advertising at cowboys; by the 1920s their jeans were becoming obligatory wear for their on-screen counterparts, worn by actors like William S. Hart and John Wayne. Before that time, few people outside of California had seen a pair of their pants. Now their increased visibility inspired new competition.

A nicely worn pair of Levi's 501 Waist Overalls from 1933. They demonstrate the standard mid-1930s features of back pocket rivets, belt loops, back cinch and no red tab; they would have been sold fitted with suspender buttons, since removed by an owner who presumably preferred belts to braces.

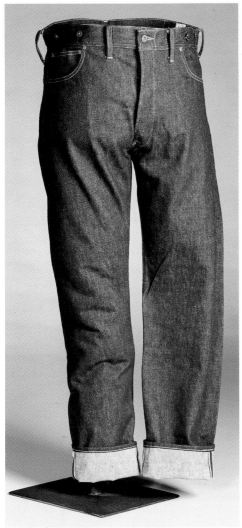 

Lee's Prestige 401 Jacket, in 13oz denim, was introduced in 1925 and with its single pocket and front pleats bore a strong resemblance to Levi's 506 jacket; this example dates from the late 1930s.

Lee's 101 Cowboy Pants, the company's definitive jeans. These pants changed considerably over the years; some examples had a Levi's-style arcuate (see overleaf); this pair, from circa 1930, has wider, dungaree-style pockets, simple back-pocket stitching and carries the early "Lee Mercantile Company" label.

These Lee 101 jeans boast the Levi's style arcuate on the back pocket, as well as rivets on the back pocket (which would of course scratch any self-respecting cowboy's saddle; very painful). Both features mark them as an early pair, dating from the 1920s. The Storm Rider jacket, introduced in 1933, would itself inspire many copies. This example, with its early housemark tag, dates from the 1930s. (Heller's Café)

NEW PATENTED LEVI'S with non-scratch CONCEALED RIVET on back pockets

X-RAY Diagram of Levi's patented concealed rivet

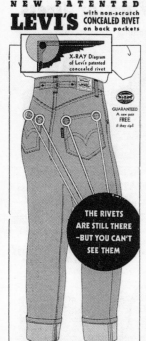

GUARANTEED
A new pair FREE if they rip!

THE RIVETS ARE STILL THERE —BUT YOU CAN'T SEE THEM

No. 501X—Boys' Sizes
26 to 29 waist
Lengths to 29 only
No. 501X $1 60
Postpaid

COWPUNCHERS' CANVAS PANTS
Heavy tan waterproof duck, corduroy trimmed, triple stitched.
30 to 42 waist
No. 444 $2 50
Postpaid

LEVI STRAUSS JACKET
No. 501J
Matches overalls. Pleated front, long sleeves. One breast pocket, tight waist.
Sizes 36 to 46
$1.80
Postpaid

MEN'S LEVI STRAUSS OVERALLS
No. 501XX
Men's Sizes
30 to 42 waist
$1.75
Postpaid

LADIES' LEVIS
No. 501L—Tailored to fit the ladies. Soft sanforized denim.
25 to 34 Waists
29 to 33 lengths
$1.75
Postage Paid

COWPUNCHERS' WATER-REPELLANT CANVAS JACKET
Tan duck corduroy trimmed. Sizes 36 to 46.
No. 445 $2 50
Postpaid

GENUINE HAIR-ON-HIDE LABEL

LEE COWBOY PANTS
The real genuine article with all the amazing improvements that make thousands buy them again and again.

6 Famous Features
1. Sanforized shrunk
2. 11½ oz. denim
3. Copper riveted strain points
4. Scratch proof hip pockets
5. U shaped saddle crotch
6. Branded hair-on-hide label

No. 101—Waist sizes 29 to 42 $1 70
Postpaid

No. 101J—Cowboy Jacket to match overalls $1 70
Sizes 34 to 44. Postpaid

FOR WINTER'S COLD
Blanket lined cowboy jacket, sizes 34 to 44, Alaskan lining.
No. 101LJ $2 85
Postpaid

LEE'S BLACK FRISCO JEANS

Made of heavy black jean cloth. Two front pockets with horizontal openings. Two hip pockets, and watch pocket. 2-inch belt loops. Adjustable waist strap in back. Cut high in back for riding comfort.

No. 721
$2 50
PER PAIR
Postpaid

Genuine Lee BOYS' COWBOY PANTS
We brand your pair with your brand or initials, or both, free of charge.

Same style that Lee makes for Western range riders. Famous Lee hair-on-hide branded label and blank hide label for the brand you select.
Size 4 to 16 years.
Per Pair, Postpaid $1 10
(Be sure to give brand)

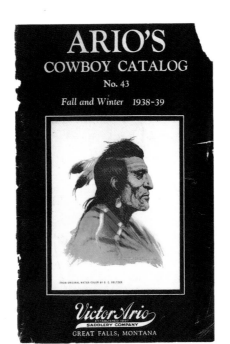

ARIO'S COWBOY CATALOG
No. 43
Fall and Winter 1938-39

FROM ORIGINAL WATER COLOR BY O. C. SELTZER

Victor Ario
SADDLERY COMPANY
GREAT FALLS, MONTANA

Around 1939, many companies offered cowboy clothes via mail order. Victor Ario, of Montana, offered both Levi's and Lee cowboy pants. Lee's entry also lists black Lee Frisco Jeans. The H.D.Lee Company bought the Eloesser-Heynemann company, owner of Can't Bust 'Em, in 1946. Frisko Jeens were one of the most popular Can't Bust 'Em products, and either inspired a Lee copy or were being bought in by Lee before it purchased the San Francisco company. Lady Levi's appeared in 1935 and were pre-shrunk Sanforized, rather than shrink-to-fit.

A pre-World War II shopfront, full of Can't Bust 'Em product, including the "Copper King Pre Shrunk Western Type Blue Denim jeans", which still sported old-fashioned suspender buttons. Far left: Can't Bust 'Em cowboy jeans ad from 1938.

Left: 501 Waist Overalls from 1939; the red tab on the back pocket was introduced in 1936, the "concealed" back rivets in 1937; the suspender buttons disappeared the same year. A pocket "flasher" and countercard advertised the fact that the back-pocket rivets were still there.

Left: Shorty Neal, one-time rider for the Pony Express, poses on his route, wearing a single-pocket Levi's 506 blouse. Above: This 506 jacket, with its red tab and earlier, silver-coloured back buckle, was made between 1936 and 1942.

Levi's had always had plenty of rivals right on its doorstep; apart from brands like Boss of the Road and Can't Bust 'Em, which each had their own distinctive product, there were many smaller competitors who'd attempted to copy its riveted pants. The response was generally a lawsuit – there was a modern zeal to Levi's efforts to wipe out counterfeit products. By 1924, however, rivals were confident that the patent on Levi's rivets had expired (in fact, although there's no conclusive evidence, it had probably run out around 1898), and introduced their own cowboy pants. In 1923 Eloesser-Heynemann was mocking the "old fashioned" rivet in its advertising. In 1924 their new riveted pants (soon to be proudly titled "Copper Kings") appeared in their price lists, along with all-black "Frisko Jeens".

Over in Kansas City, H.D. Lee Mercantile Co. had always produced its own waistband overalls; its main model was the 11W, but it had never enjoyed the popularity of Lee's bib overalls. All of that was to change with the company's own "101 Cowboy Waistband Overalls". Probably introduced in 1924, they were first mentioned in the price lists for the company's San Francisco outlet in 1925, but it would be another four or five years before they were listed in all of Lee's territories.

In many respects, those first 101s were an unashamed attempt to muscle in on Levi's territory. They featured copper rivets, the basic cut was similar to that of Levi's 501 and many early examples featured the "double arcuate" stitching on the back pockets which had become synonymous with Levi's. As time went on, Lee's cowboy pants became more distinctive; a deeper yoke (the triangular section above the pockets) and a "U-shaped Saddle Crotch" made them comfier when riding a horse. Lee introduced a zipper-fly version, the 1010, as early as 1925; it was later retitled the 101Z. Whereas Levi's distribution was essentially confined to the West Coast, Lee jeans were strong in the Midwest and the East; the company soon claimed to be selling more pants to cowboys than Levi's. The company's first cowboy jackets also bore a strong resemblance to contemporary Levi's, but by 1932, when Lee introduced its Slim 101J jacket, the company was no longer content to copy its competitors. Levi's own 506 jacket, or blouse overall, was pleated and comparatively baggy; Lee's was shorter,

Above and right: Proof that they do make 'em bigger in Texas. Big Tex, the 52-foot tall symbol of the State Fair of Texas, made his debut in 1952, and the Lee company made his oversize duds for the next 40 years.

Lee's 131 Cowboy Pants were a budget version of the 101. In a lighter 8oz denim, they featured a more old-fashioned dungaree cut. This pair was produced in the 1930s.

The H.D. Lee Company was using Sanforized non-shrink denim by the 1930s. This series of advertisements, from the hand of in-house advertising artist Chester Blueman, includes a rare appearance of Lee's 101J slimline jacket.

snugger and sexier, just the thing for cowboys. It was doubtless a substantial influence on Levi's own 557 Trucker jacket, produced nearly three decades later.

Lee wasn't the only company trespassing on Levi's home territory. By the mid-1930s, many major denim makers were offering products that resembled the 501. JC Penney had its own Foremost brand aimed at cowboys, while OshKosh, Washington Dee Cee and many major names offered their own riveted pants.

If Levi's had been subjected to such intense competition earlier, the company might well have been forced to close down. After Levi's death in 1902, the business passed into the hands of his sister's sons, Jacob, Louis, Abraham and Sigmund Stern. In 1919 Sigmund asked his new son-in-law Walter Haas to join the business, which by then was ailing. Haas turned the company around, not least by his insistence on spending unthinkable sums on advertising, even in the mid-1920s when cotton prices dropped and the US clothing industry was in turmoil. Haas continued the tradition, established by Levi, of accentuating the product's "brand values". Compared to its competition,

The 101J was arguably Lee's first truly original article of cowboy clothing; this example dates from the 1950s. The slimline look of the 101J influenced Levi's 557XX Trucker jacket and many other more literal imitations.

Levi's image and advertising was slicker and more clearly differentiated. When other manufacturers started producing riveted clothing, Levi's responded by adding yet another visual device to brand their product: the red tab. Introduced in 1936, it was the brainchild of sales manager Chris Lucier. It was intended as a foolproof method of identifying the definitive brand of riveted pants, and so it remains today. Some purchasers might wonder why it's possible to buy the odd pair of Levi's that features a blank red tab without the Levi's name. The reason? It's a trademark gambit, to register the distinctive nature of the red tab alone as opposed to the Levi's name that it carries.

If anyone doubted that the heyday of the cowboy was finally over, perhaps the most conclusive evidence came in the form of the "Dude Ranches", which started springing up over California and Nevada in the 1930s. Designed for city slickers to get a taste of life on the trail, it was the perfect product placement for Levi's, which by 1938 had introduced a wide range of Dude Ranch Duds. The "High colour Rodeo and Fiesta shirts" hardly epitomized the tough, labourers' practicality that Levi Strauss and Jacob Davis had championed. But they signalled the company's unconscious, telepathic ability of being at the centre of every new social trend.

Levi Strauss & Co. was producing a wide range of Dude Ranch clothing by 1938. The catalogue featured a new Dude Ranch jacket, the "Riders", plus a range of "High Colour Rodeo and Fiesta Shirts".

Arthur Rothstein, like Dorothea Lange, was a photographer for the Farm Security Administration and captured many haunting dust bowl images. Rancher Walter Latta, of Bozeman, Montana, was photographed in July 1939 in classic western garb, including a two-pocket generic jacket, clearly based on the design of Levi's 506.

FROM WARTIME TO PLAYTIME
Denim becomes the uniform of war and peace

As Europe was engulfed by war in 1939, the USA seemed self-consciously estranged; countless popular hillbilly songs warned the country's rulers to devote themselves to helping struggling farmers rather than embattled Europeans. Six years later, America emerged from a global war as the world's greatest superpower. American values – and products – would permeate the world. In the process, America's archetypal clothing would undergo its own transformation.

There were few clues to this socio-economic revolution in 1939, as the nation's denim industry continued to cater for workers and aspiring cowboys. Levi Strauss & Co. was still dominant on the West Coast, while the H.D. Lee Mercantile Company celebrated its 50th anniversary by announcing that, with annual sales of $6.4 million, it was now the country's biggest workwear manufacturer. Sales of its bib overalls were booming; the cowboy market was also proving highly lucrative. Among denim fetishists, Lee cowboy pants of the late 1930s and early 1940s boast the ultimate cachet, signalled by a Hair On Hide patch, each one branded by hand on to a piece of cowhide. In 1941 Lee revised the fit of its cowboy jeans with the aid of rodeo star Turk Greenough and his "exotic fan dancer" wife, Sally Rand. During a visit to Lee's headquarters in Kansas City, Rand picked apart a pair of the company's cowboy jeans and had them retailored to a tighter fit, along with a slight flare for Turk's boots. This style would immediately become de rigueur for cowboys, and would one day become known as a "boot cut".

Of course, this last cowboy idyll would end with America's entry to the war, as every denim manufacturer was asked to do its patriotic duty. In the case of Levi's, a

A "morale-boosting" advertisement for Blue Bell. The company supplied clothing to the services, but was also a huge workwear manufacturer, making brands like Blue Bell and Casey Jones and supplying retail chains such as JC Penney.

Lee Hair On Hide 101 cowboy pants from circa 1939. They feature arcuate stitching on the back pocket similar to that of Levi's, as well as the classic cowhide label. The quintessential early cowboy pants, these are among the most collectable Lee jeans and are now available in a replica version via Edwin, Lee's licensee in Japan.

Opposite: A Navy maintenance crew wrestle with an F6F Grumman Hellcat on the US Lexington, 1943, in the Pacific. Denim Bell Bottoms were first specified by the US Navy in 1901; dozens of large and small companies manufactured them during World War II.

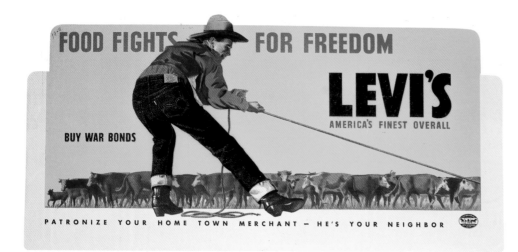

FOOD FIGHTS FOR FREEDOM
BUY WAR BONDS
LEVI'S
AMERICA'S FINEST OVERALL
PATRONIZE YOUR HOME TOWN MERCHANT – HE'S YOUR NEIGHBOR

As a comparatively small clothing company, Levi Strauss & Co. only won minor military contracts. But as this wartime ad illustrates, cowboys contributed to the war effort, too.

Wartime cutbacks contributed to the development of modern Levi's jeans. The buckleback disappeared for ever; the distinctive arcuate stitching was replaced by the painted version (above), which normally disappeared after a couple of washes. The stitching returned in 1947. Like other military clothing, prisoner-of-war issue denim was manufactured by many different companies. This pair dates from the 1930s. (Heller's Café)

comparatively small manufacturer, that duty was mainly confined to minimizing consumption of material vital to the war effort, which included copper – and cotton. For the only time in the company's history, the copper rivets disappeared, replaced by steel rivets with a copper wash. The War Production Board also decided that Levi's arcuate stitching constituted a wasteful use of cotton, and the company instead introduced a simple printed imitation. The buckle back disappeared too, never to return.

Although there's long been a tradition that Levi's supplied denim wear to the US Navy, this seems to have no basis in fact. The company itself believes its only government contract was fur-lined parkas for Alaskan troops, according to Walter Haas, Jr, son of the then Managing Director of the company. Instead, Levi's main patriotic effect was to improve the morale of US servicemen who, according to many letters home, slept with their precious jeans under their pillow, probably because if they were stolen there was only a remote possibility of being able to buy another pair.

Right: Norman Rockwell's illustration of Rosie The Riveter for the cover of The Saturday Evening Post perfectly captured the contribution women (clad in denim, naturally) made to the war effort.

No Question About It...

(The cowboy is Casey Tibbs, World's Champion Cowboy)

Lee is your best value in work clothes

America's Best-Made, Best-Known Work Clothes

Union Made. Buy them at leading retail stores coast to coast.

Wartime restrictions meant the Levi's 506 jacket of the time was simplified in design, most notably with the loss of the flap on the single breast pocket. This jacket also features simpler "doughnut" buttons with a laurel wreath design (see also the buttons on Marlon Brando's 501 jeans, page 1).

The Wrangler name was purchased by the Blue Bell corporation in 1943. It would soon be put to use on the company's successful range of cowboy clothing.

Denim workwear had been just about as ubiquitous within the US military as it was in the civilian population; denim bell bottoms were first approved for US Navy use in 1901. Although many companies, including Eloesser-Heynemann, produced Bell Bottoms in small numbers, Bell Bottom manufacture during World War II was dominated by traditional military suppliers such as the Polkton Manufacturing Company of Marshville, North Carolina, which produced Seafarer Bell Bottoms. Much of the denim for these pants was "818" or Jelt from Cone, which at that time was also producing Levi's denim – perhaps the reason for apocryphal stories of Levi's links with the Navy. Cone subsequently received the Army-Navy "E" Award for its work towards the war effort.

Meanwhile, a fast-growing future rival of Levi's was becoming the biggest workwear manufacturer to supply America's armed forces. The Blue Bell Overall Company, of Greensboro, North Carolina and the Globe Superior corporation had merged in 1936,

Casey Tibbs & Lee Dealer
[in Tom's ... N.J. about 195...]

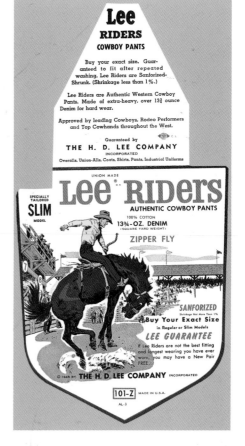

Lee's 101 Cowboy Pants were renamed Lee Riders around 1944; they gained the "Lazy S" stitching used to this day and changed considerably in shape to become the forerunner of today's boot-cut jeans, with a tighter fit around the thigh, together with a modest flare. Here Casey Tibbs, "World Champion Cowboy", poses with a Lee dealer in New Jersey in 1950; at this time, Lee had little competition in the cowboy market outside California. Tibbs was a fixture in Lee's advertising campaign (far left).

purchased the H.D. Bob Company in 1940, and then acquired the Casey Jones Company of Baltimore, Maryland – owner of the then little-used name "Wrangler" – in 1943. In its factories all over the south, Blue Bell Inc produced over 24 million items of military clothing. Over in Kansas, the H.D. Lee Company also produced fatigues, jackets and flight suits for the US military – but presciently maintained its advertising for its workwear and cowboy pants range, all of it aimed at civilians who quite possibly couldn't even get hold of the product.

By 1945 Lee was well placed to benefit from a profound social shift. Within a few years workwear would cease to be the company's primary focus. Instead, a world of leisure was beckoning. In 1946 Lee purchased Eloesser-Heynemann, which now owned both the Can't Bust 'Em and Boss of the Road brands. Can't Bust 'Em's Frisko Jeens were the definitive black denim pants on the West Coast, and were immediately adopted into Lee's range. The company's San Francisco factory was turned over to Lee

Hollywood's stars continued to provide invaluable product placement for denim manufacturers throughout the war; here Gary Cooper models a chambray shirt for Glamour magazine, 1940. (Alexander Paal)

products, most notably its 101 Cowboy Pants, now known as Lee Riders.

Another telling sign of the times came in 1947, when Blue Bell Inc changed its slogan from "The World's Biggest Producer Of Work Clothes" to "The World's Biggest Producer of Work *And Play* Clothes". It wasn't simply bravado. With the help of Philadelphia Western clothing designer "Rodeo Ben", the company had produced its own range of cowboy pants and jackets, reviving the Wrangler name. Made of 11oz Sanforized denim, the jeans featured a plastic label – which wouldn't stick to a leather saddle – and soon became one of Blue Bell's biggest lines.

Even as its rivals turned from bib overalls to "jeans", competing directly with its prime product, Levi Strauss & Co. was about to undergo a seismic corporate shift. The company's managing director, Walter Haas, had come under pressure from wartime authorities to compromise standards by reducing the weight of the denim used in the 501 and other jeans. He had refused outright. Meanwhile, his customers had become the biggest evangelists for Levi's products, and in the social melting pot cooked up by a world war, Levi's was about to change from a Californian institution into an all-American one. And as an all-American institution, its appeal would soon reach worldwide.

Cowboy outfit: Wrangler's first cowboy gear appeared in the form of 1947's **11MW** jeans and 1948's **11MJ** jacket. The 11MJ jacket featured distinctive front pleats. Early versions featured vents on the shoulder allowing for more freedom of movement; they are missing on this example. The **11MWZ** jeans shown date from the 1950s. (Heller's Café)

WHAT'VE YOU GOT?
Rebels, rockabillies and other menaces to society

In 1953 the H.D. Lee Company started to take out advertisements directed at its teenage clients. They featured photos of two boys sitting at their school desks: one was freshly scrubbed, his jeans with perfect turn-ups, his posture perfect. Above his photo there was a heading: "the right way".

The boy's evil alter ego slouched under the legend "the wrong way". His fringe flopped down, his jeans were askew. One sneakered foot was insolently pushed out from under the desk, his books lay scattered and ignored.

Around the country millions of teenagers were pondering the choices represented by the Lee advertisement. Thousands of them decided to opt for the wrong way.

For many outraged parents there was one evil proselytizer responsible for sending their kids to the dark side: Elvis Presley, who first registered on America's consciousness with That's All Right Mama in 1954. Yet although Elvis embodied teenage rebellion, he didn't spread the denim look. Schooled at first hand in the black music of Memphis, Tennessee, he instinctively adopted the attitudes of black musicians who would never wear jeans on-stage; denim reminded them of cotton fields and sharecropping. Little Milton Campbell was, and still is, one of the big names in the Memphis music scene – Elvis would regularly watch him play at Tippy's in Marks, Mississippi. He remains outraged at the concept of a musician wearing denim on-stage: "So many entertainers help to stereotype themselves by not bringing a change of

Levi's 507 jacket – "Number 2" to collectors – debuted in 1953; it featured two pockets and side straps, rather than the back cinch of its predecessor.

Eddie Cochran made a crucial contribution to Levi's mythology, partly because he was often seen in 501s and matching 506 jacket. The story of his love affair with co-writer Sharon Sheeley was immortalised in a 1980s UK TV commercial; after pondering the best outfit to wear for meeting Eddie, Sharon opted for a pair of Levi's – and got her guy. (Courtesy Julie Monday, from Don't Forget Me, The Eddie Cochran story.)

clothes to their performance. Those people who think you got to be funky and stinky, you got to wear raggety jeans... to me that's the wrong concept!" Elvis agreed, and while he might have worn Levi's off-stage, he only wore denim in a professional capacity when instructed to do so by a Hollywood wardrobe department; as in, for instance, 1957's Loving You.

Instead, it would be a different tradition that clad rock'n'roll in denim; one personified by Eddie Cochran. Cochran grew up in Minnesota; he didn't hear black music first-hand in the way Elvis did, and instead grew up schooled in country – state-of-the-art country, not the hillbilly version you'd hear down in Mississippi. Cochran was a skilled studio musician who worked country sessions before he turned to rock 'n' roll, and his sense of style came straight from the local cowboy scene. Fatefully, he was a Levi's man.

Officially, Levi's pants weren't even available outside the West Coast until the opening of a New York State outlet in 1949, but mail-order Westernwear catalogues were promoting Levi's as the definitive cowboy jeans as early as 1938. It was possibly from such a source that Eddie Cochran bought his first Levi's outfit. By 1951 Eddie moved to LA and would effectively prototype the rockabilly look; others like Ronnie Dawson, Duane Eddy – and even 1980s rockabilly Brian Seltzer – would soon follow.

Cochran – and thousands of other rockabillies – showed that the impact of Levi's jeans was about to permeate the Midwest. But in California, where riveted jeans were born, they were already a fixture. One of the most crucial moments in the mythology of denim took place when John Garfield turned down the lead in Elia Kazan's production of

Top: Art Taylor, musician and biker, at Hines Farm, a juke joint and the home of Atomic Pirate motorcycle club – "the oldest black motorcycle club in the country". He's wearing black denim pants, probably Lee's popular Frisco Jeans. (Courtesy Matthew Donahue)

Above: Bikers, Santa Clara, California, 1947. Many bikers were fresh out of the services, and traded in their uniform "for a leather jacket and a pair of Levi's".

Opposite: Elvis meets his fans, 1957. Elvis was rarely seen in public wearing denim in the 1950s; he associated workwear with the poverty of his youth.

Lowell Dicey (top left) was a typical Navy man, ex-intelligence, who bought a Harley straight after demobilization and attended the legendary 1947 Hollister "riot". These 1949 photos show him at another biker celebration at La Grange, California, with sister Carol and friends Ally Gonzales and Don Barnes. "We *all* wore Levi's," Carol remembered recently. (Courtesy Dennis Alstrand). Opposite: Marlon Brando in Levi's and leather on the set of The Wild One. Based on the events of Hollister, Stanley Kramer's movie unwittingly inspired a new generation of biker rebels.

Above left: Cool-school trumpeter Chet Baker was briefly imprisoned in Lucca, Italy for drug offences in 1961. The experience failed to cramp his style; here he's decorating a Christmas tree, wearing Levi's for the occasion.

Above: Norman Mailer published his iconoclastic anti-war novel The Naked And The Dead in 1948, based on his service in the Pacific campaign. His denim-clad, tough-guy persona underlined his belief that his rival writers were effete and irrelevant.

Left: A stunning pair of Levi's 501 pants from the 1950s. The leather patch would disappear by the end of the decade.

Tennessee Williams' play A Streetcar Named Desire in the summer of 1947. Williams' agent suggested a young actor called Marlon Brando for the lead role. Brando arrived for a reading; he fixed the lights and the plumbing, according to Williams, before convincing the playwright he was "a God-sent Stanley Kowalski". On Broadway that December, then in Elia Kazan's movie of 1951, Brando signalled the emergence of a new breed of actor. The wartime Levi's Brando was wearing would become iconic along with the man; James Dean, Montgomery Clift and Paul Newman would become denim-clad icons in Brando's wake.

Mickey Spillane, author of many best-selling hard-boiled detective novels including Kiss Me Deadly. Spillane believed most of the actors who essayed the role of his best-known creation, Mike Hammer, were inadequate, and that he could do a better job. This photo of him at home in Levi's and white T-shirt in April 1953 suggests he did at least have more charisma than most of the screen Hammers.

Lee ad campaign aimed at African American teenagers from 1953. They illustrate how Lee Riders changed to a "drainpipe" shape in the 1950s. The distinctive selvage edges of Lee jeans disappeared gradually during the 1950s, early jeans boasted a double selvage, most 1950s jeans had selvage on merely one edge of the fabric; the selvage was completely gone by 1958.

Brando signalled a profound change in the direction denim's image was taking. This was far removed from the all-American hero image represented by cowboys or loco workers. There was more than a hint of rough trade in Stanley Kowalski – hardly surprising, given he was based on Williams' current flame – and Williams, himself not averse to camping it up in bell bottoms while sojourning in California, was well aware of the rude appeal of Brando's greasy jeans and grubby vest.

Stanley's rude appeal was counterpointed by the play's lyrical undertow – its regretful noting of the passing of Southern gentility – but Brando's next movie was less subtle fare. It was based around an infamous incident that took place in the summer that Streetcar's cast were rehearsing.

On 4 July 1947 a group of motorcyclists descended on the quiet California town of Hollister for a Gypsy Tour Celebration rally and hill-climb. Few accounts agree as to what happened next; there was either some random carousing or a full-scale riot in which a biker gang armed with crowbars busted several of their friends from the city jail. The San Francisco Chronicle sent a photographer down to depict the mayhem; he returned with a shot showing a drunken biker slumped over his Harley Knucklehead, surrounded by empty beer bottles. According to the bikers the shot was posed using a portly local resident and a borrowed motorcycle. In any case, when the photograph was reproduced on the cover of Life magazine on 21 July, it caused uproar. Most of America agreed with the Hollister resident who termed the visitors "lawless, drunken, filthy bands of motorcycle fiends", and debated the cause of such degeneracy.

Many observers speculated that the troublesome motorcycle thugs were ex-servicemen unable to settle down. That was partly true, at least in the case of Wino Willie Forkner, who attend the Hollister rally with the Boozefighters, a motorcycling club

James Dean famously wore Lee jeans in his best-known movies such as Rebel without A Cause (his adversary, Corey Allen wore Levi's). Levi Strauss & Co.'s company lore is that Dean was actually a Levi's fan; sadly, this photo of him at the family farm doesn't reveal which side of the denim divide he belonged to; he's wearing cheap workwear pants and a Wrangler-influenced, blanket-lined zip jacket.

Levi Strauss & Co. introduced a number of Western shirts around 1938, but as far as many collectors are concerned, the company's definitive shirt arrived in 1954: the Sawtooth, named for the shape of the pocket flaps.

formed in South Central Los Angeles in 1946, mostly comprising ex-servicemen. "In the early days of biking, they immediately thought you were an outlaw sort of person. We didn't think we were. We didn't go around banging heads," Willie told the San Francisco Chronicle. "We were rebelling against the establishment, for Chrissakes. You go fight a goddamn war, and the minute you get back and take off the uniform and put on Levi's and leather jackets, they call you an asshole!"

When director Stanley Kramer decided to film John Paxton's script, based on the Hollister incident, he changed many details in an effort to add romance and a moral to the tale. He kept the detail of the Levi's and the leather jackets.

The Wild Ones wasn't Marlon Brando's finest acting moment; the movie's "hep-talk", its desire to "understand" rendered it formulaic rather than profound. But the perfection of its imagery was obvious, and although Marlon wasn't supposed to be a role model, a generation of youths decided to buy a leather jacket and a pair of Levi's – which were then, fortunately, becoming readily available across the country. At the same time, Levi's dropped the description "Waist Overalls", acknowledging the fact that its customers were calling its product "jeans".

Levi's jeans rode the crest of a new wave of youth culture; so did Lee, whose 101 Riders were worn by James Dean in his two most famous movies, Rebel Without A

By the late 1950s, Wrangler had taken a huge slice of the cowboy market. As far as Hollywood was concerned, however, standard cowboy wear comprised Levi 501s and Lee Storm Rider jacket. Here Kirk Douglas, in Lonely Are The Brave, and Paul Newman, in Hud, sport the obligatory denim combination.

Far left: Marilyn Monroe relaxes in Levi's on the set of The Misfits. Monroe would also help make Lee's Storm Rider (left) famous. The blanket-lined (or "Alaskan Lining") version of the 101J, with a corduroy collar, it was introduced in 1933 and has remained in the company's range ever since. This example dates from the 1950s. (Heller's Café)

Far left, bottom photo: Levi's jeans first major European market seems to have been France; here Brigitte Bardot reclines in a pair of 501s. Gina Lollobrigida, meanwhile, wears Italian-made pedalpushers (below).

Cause and Giant. Even JC Penney benefited; its Foremost jeans were affordable versions of the big two's incendiary originals. When Marilyn Monroe was photographed wearing a pair of Penney's Foremost they acquired an extra frisson. Yet even as these companies were benefiting from this cultural explosion, they remained ambivalent about their own image and – as with Lee's advertising campaign – attempted to portray themselves as the choice of socially responsible young adults.

Levi Strauss & Co launched an advertisement in 1957 with similar aims to that of Lee's earlier campaign. Picturing a clean-cut boy wearing Levi's, it was titled "Right for school". Few parents were convinced; one New Jersey woman wrote to the company to complain: "While I have to admit that this may be 'right for school' in San Francisco, in the West, or in some rural areas, I can assure you that it is in bad taste and not right for school in the East and particularly New York. Of course, you may have different standards and perhaps your employees are permitted to wear Bermuda shorts or golf togs in your office while transacting Levi's business!"

As Lynn Downey, Historian in charge of Levi Strauss & Co.'s archives observes dryly, "Interesting, isn't it, how this woman predicted the future trend toward casual clothing in the workplace?"

Neal and Carolyn Cassady check out the wares in a used car lot, San Francisco, late 1947. "Ever since I met him in March 1947 I never saw him in anything but Levi's until his death in February 1969," remembers Carolyn today. "He may have worn chinos or something elsewhere, but I only saw him in Levi's, and he had nothing else in *our* closet!" The Beats were widely regarded as responsible for the spread of the denim look, although Cassady, who appeared as "Dean Moriarty" in Kerouac's On The Road, was the only one ever seen in public in Levi's.

INTELLECTUALS WITH ATTITUDE
Denim becomes the uniform of the counterculture

"Jack Kerouac was responsible for selling a million pairs of jeans with On The Road," his fellow writer Williams Burroughs theorized in 1969. Burroughs was well aware that none of the participants in Kerouac's manifesto for the beat movement, published in 1957, actually wore jeans at the time. In Burroughs' mind, Kerouac had created a new American aesthetic, in which the ubiquity of denim became inevitable.

Kerouac was, of course, only one of a cast of thousands responsible for this growth. In retrospect, the true miracle of the fabric's spread was the way it seemed to exemplify countless lifestyles – many of them mutually exclusive. In the Midwest jeans represented the all-American hero, the cowboy, right through to the 1960s. In California they represented miners, mechanics and people who tinkered with Harley Davidsons; it would take decades before they'd be accepted by Kerouac's followers and fans. In New York, however, jeans were seen as synonymous with intellectuals and the counterculture as early as the 1940s.

When Time magazine featured the artist Jackson Pollock in 1948, they derisively termed him "Jack The Dripper". Life magazine was more supportive and in August 1949 ran a profile that asked the question, "Is he the greatest living painter in the United States?". For the interview Pollock donned tweed coat and polished loafers, but when he arrived at Arnold Newman's studio for the photoshoot he dressed "in character". Wearing dark, paint-splattered denim, he stared thuggishly at the camera, signalling that art was no longer the province of suited, effete intellectuals. One year later, Hans

Jackson Pollock poses in his East Hampton studio for his landmark feature in Life Magazine, August 1949. "The blue-collar duds, the defiant swagger, the surly squinting stare-down would launch a thousand imitators," says Kirk Varnedoe, Chief Curator, New York Museum Of Modern Art.

Jackson Pollock's blue-collar denim look (page 81) may well have derived from Picasso (pictured top left by Lee Miller), but it became de rigueur in the art community as Andy Warhol, Peter Blake, Max Ernst (shown in his Huismes studio, 1955) and Willem de Kooning demonstrate, shown clockwise from top right. Levi's seemed to be the obligatory label; Warhol's jeans, just to be different, were invariably black, but they were still Levi's, according to Factory insiders. Willem de Kooning could, however, be seen sporting Washington Dee Cee overalls in his studio.

Bob Dylan, civil rights activist, plays on the back porch of the SNCC offices, Greenwood Mississippi, 1963. Bob Dylan's early persona was heavily influenced by dustbowl balladeer Woody Guthrie; there was also more than a passing nod to the influence of Kerouac and the Beats. It was therefore inevitable that, like his fellow Greenwich Village folkies, Bob was invariably seen in denim (or cords) in his pre-electric era.

Some artists don't simply wear denim. Joseph Beuys has frequently used denim in his work as part of collages, such as 1984's La Jambe d'Orwell.

By the 1950s, Levi's jeans had spread beyond their original Californian heartland, and the selection of products expanded (the full range of men's jeans is shown left). The 1960s 501s shown here feature the "leather look" label, made of pressed card, which debuted towards the end of the 1950s.

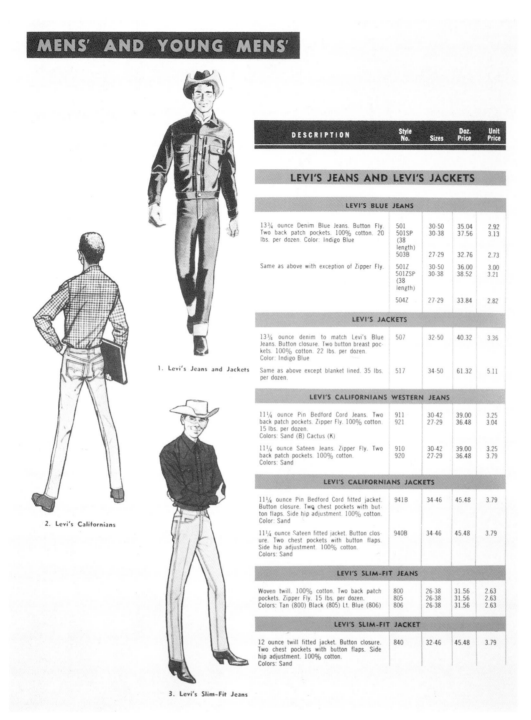

DESCRIPTION	Style No.	Sizes	Doz. Price	Unit Price
LEVI'S JEANS AND LEVI'S JACKETS				
LEVI'S BLUE JEANS				
13¾ ounce Denim Blue Jeans. Button Fly. Two back patch pockets. 100% cotton. 20 lbs. per dozen. Color: Indigo Blue	501	30-50	35.04	2.92
	501SP (38 length)	30-38	37.56	3.13
	503B	27-29	32.76	2.73
Same as above with exception of Zipper Fly.	501Z	30-50	36.00	3.00
	501ZSP (38 length)	30-38	38.52	3.21
	504Z	27-29	33.84	2.82
LEVI'S JACKETS				
13¾ ounce denim to match Levi's Blue Jeans. Button closure. Two button breast pockets. 100% cotton. 22 lbs. per dozen. Color: Indigo Blue	507	32-50	40.32	3.36
Same as above except blanket lined. 35 lbs. per dozen.	517	34-50	61.32	5.11
LEVI'S CALIFORNIANS WESTERN JEANS				
11¼ ounce Pin Bedford Cord Jeans. Two back patch pockets. Zipper Fly. 100% cotton. 15 lbs. per dozen. Colors: Sand (B) Cactus (K)	911	30-42	39.00	3.25
	921	27-29	36.48	3.04
11¼ ounce Sateen Jeans. Zipper Fly. Two back patch pockets. 100% cotton. Colors: Sand	910	30-42	39.00	3.25
	920	27-29	36.48	3.79
LEVI'S CALIFORNIANS JACKETS				
11¼ ounce Pin Bedford Cord fitted jacket. Button closure. Two chest pockets with button flaps. Side hip adjustment. 100% cotton. Color: Sand	941B	34-46	45.48	3.79
11¼ ounce Sateen fitted jacket. Button closure. Two chest pockets with button flaps. Side hip adjustment. 100% cotton. Colors: Sand	940B	34-46	45.48	3.79
LEVI'S SLIM-FIT JEANS				
Woven twill. 100% cotton. Two back patch pockets. Zipper Fly. 15 lbs. per dozen. Colors: Tan (800) Black (805) Lt. Blue (806)	800	26-38	31.56	2.63
	805	26-38	31.56	2.63
	806	26-38	31.56	2.63
LEVI'S SLIM-FIT JACKET				
12 ounce twill fitted jacket. Button closure. Two chest pockets with button flaps. Side hip adjustment. 100% cotton. Colors: Sand	840	32-46	45.48	3.79

1. Levi's Jeans and Jackets

2. Levi's Californians

3. Levi's Slim-Fit Jeans

Namuth filmed a series of arresting action sequences of Pollock at work in his East Hampton studio. Splashing paint over a glass plate, dressed in Levi's 501s and Lee 101 jacket, possessed of a hypnotic, fevered energy, he created a new template for the way an artist should look. Before long, other painters such as Willem de Kooning – who'd regularly venture out with Pollock to see jazz iconoclasts like Miles Davis and John Coltrane – and Roy Lichtenstein were being photographed in paint-splattered Levi's. The moment he or she donned a pair of jeans, the intellectual became a battle-hardened, no-nonsense tough guy. European-influenced writers, such as Saul Bellow, wore suits for their magazine profiles; all-American bruisers like Norman Mailer would stare at the camera with the same bedenimed, battle-scarred pose as Pollock.

Although the rock'n'roll denim look made tentative inroads into Europe in the 1950s,

Right: From the 1950s onwards, denim built up an elusive cachet, becoming a badge of cool in often mutually exclusive cultures. Cary Grant, at least in public, was the epitome of the safe Hollywood establishment. Naturally, posing for GQ in Palm Springs in 1964 he chose to wear denim, including a "sawtooth"-style Western shirt.

THE FASHION MAGAZINE FOR MEN   MARCH 1964   ONE DOLLAR

GQ
GENTLEMEN'S QUARTERLY

GQ
visits
CG
in Palm Springs

california...
a clothes and culture
roundup

Steve McQueen, photographed by William Claxton in Columbus, Texas, 1963. Clad in Levi's pants and Wrangler Western shirt, much like Cary Grant, he nonetheless signalled the ascendance of a new Hollywood aristocracy. Paul Newman, generally dressed in Lee Riders by Hollywood's wardrobe departments, opted for genuine cowboy Wrangler jeans when photographed with Lee Marvin on the set of Pocket Money by Terry O'Neill.

as homegrown heroes like France's Johnny Hallyday donned expensive imported Levi's ensembles, it was the UK's art-college scene that picked up on the tradition established by Pollock and his fellow Abstract Expressionists. The painter Peter Blake – known to the wider world via his design for the Beatles' Sergeant Pepper sleeve – remembers, "I first saw a pair of Levi's in about 1947 or 1948 when a sculpture teacher came back from America with a pair, but it wasn't until the early '60s I took ownership of a pair. That was how scarce they were."

Throughout the early 1960s, art students would travel up to Laurence Corner, a workwear and army surplus store in London's Euston, to try and track down Levi's. "Laurence Corner was the only place that had them," remembers Miles, who later ran the Indica Gallery and Bookshop – the seminal location of London's counterculture in the 1960s and, incidentally, the place where John Lennon met Yoko Ono. "They didn't always have Levi's, and sometimes you'd go up there and they'd only have absolutely huge sizes in stock."

By 1964, English mods had decided that a pair of Levi's 501s with turnups was the obligatory accompaniment to a Lambretta scooter and a collection of Tamla Motown singles, but within 12 months, tastes had moved on, in favour of white Lee Westerner jeans and jackets, which had debuted on the American market in 1959 and were now being imported by an enterprising Army & Navy store in Aldgate, London (tales of mods buying jeans from American sailors are largely apocryphal). "The white Levi's were revolutionary," remembers Kenny Jones, of London's definitive mod band, the Small

Faces, "before long everyone was wearing them." Levi's introduced its own white jeans range, initially under the Slim Fit label, in 1960, and these, too, were imported in ever-increasing numbers, soon to be followed by Levi's Sta-Prest pants, and the Lee equivalent, Lee-Prest, both introduced in 1964. The Small Faces and their mass-market mod rivals, The Who, were both photographed in all-white Lee or Levi ensembles. Rivals such as the Stones and The Beatles, meanwhile, opted for more conventional suits, at least until the opening of the first Levi Strauss outlet on London's Kings Road, around 1968; John Lennon and George Harrison would soon be seen in jeans and denim jackets.

By 1965, Levi Strauss & Co., Lee and Wrangler were enjoying an unprecedented sales boom – the H.D. Lee Company opened no less than six new plants in the mid-'60s to cope with demand. The shape of each company's jeans had evolved over the years: Levi's 501 and Lee's 101 had changed to a narrower, drainpipe shape in the 1960s. Wrangler, which by now dominated the cowboy market, retained the boot cut shape introduced by Westernwear consultant Rodeo Ben back in 1948. All three companies, their marketing campaigns would suggest, envisaged that Sta-Prest and other similar more preppie looks would be their major growth area. Once again, their own consumers would surprise them, as a new generation opted for old-fashioned denim.

By 1966, Levi Strauss's West Coast location once again proved fateful, as a new generation of psychedelic rockers based themselves in Haight-Ashbury. San Francisco-based photographers such as Baron Wolman and Robert Altman captured images of seemingly every major band – Jefferson Airplane, Big Brother And The Holding Company, Grateful Dead, Santana – clad in Levi's, and as Hollywood tuned in to hippy culture, a new generation of movie stars such as Dennis Hopper and Peter Fonda dressed themselves in Levi's 501s and the company's slimline 557 Trucker jacket. The combination of the company's boot cut jeans, introduced in 1969, with the 557 would

By 1970 Marvin Gaye (top left), frustrated by the restrictions of record label Motown, rebelled by recording his "political" album, What's Going On, smoking dope and wearing denim – equally radical statements, given that African American performers had previously associated denim with poverty and sharecropping. Encouraged by wife Betty, Miles Davis (top right), dressed in denim in 1968 for his electric Newport appearance. Beatle John Lennon also donned denim that year, acquiring Levi's and a Wrangler jacket (right) during the recording of The Beatles. Levi's 517 Saddleman jeans of 1969 (above) signalled the rise of the boot cut shape.

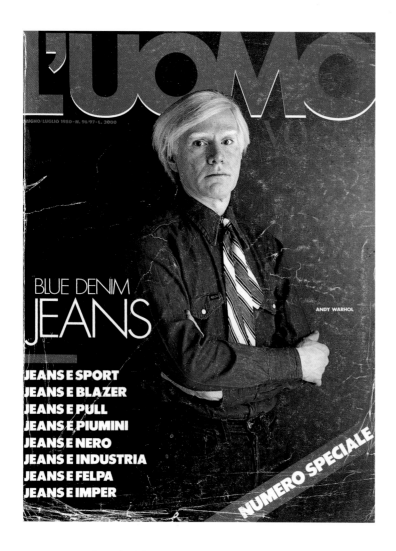

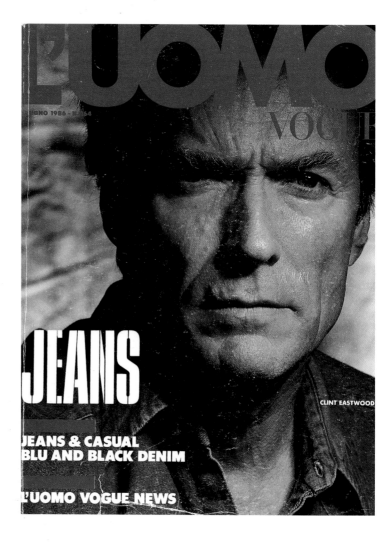

create another fashion staple, which would spread to Detroit's proto-punk scene in 1969 (and would crop up again in England in the mid-1990s, with bands like Oasis). By Woodstock, in 1969 (and the festival's nemesis, Altamont, in 1970), denim had become the uniform of the counterculture. Except, by now, the counterculture had become *the* culture. Denim was by now the world's most popular fabric, yet somehow it still retained its rebel status.

From the 1970s on, denim became truly ubiquitous; the big American manufacturers were now turning out millions of jeans, both in the USA and Europe. In contrast to the simple choice of three major models of 1950, the customer could choose from literally hundreds of alternative shapes and finishes.

By 1975, blue jeans as a symbol of rebellion should have been extinct. Then a small clique of New York musicians started to congregate around a small Bowery bar called CBGB. The most popular band on the scene was called Television; its bassist, Richard Hell, devised a radical new look, cropping his hair short and ripping his T-shirts – and his jeans. Malcolm McLaren, over in New York with the intention of reviving the post-glam, pre-punk act New York Dolls, took note, and would soon recreate Hell's ripped-clothes aesthetic, via his King's Road shop, with Vivienne Westwood – and the next band he managed. They were called the Sex Pistols.

Richard Hell's style was simplified and stripped down by another bunch of Television fans who called themselves The Ramones. Their manager, Danny Fields, had helped

What was cool in Hollywood and New York in the 1940s remained fashionable in Europe four decades later, as Andy Warhol and Clint Eastwood become cover stars of special denim issues of L'Uomo Vogue in 1980 and 1986 respectively.

Lee's Rainbow Jeans were introduced in 1976 to use up the factory's surplus coloured thread. Sales were uninspiring until Lee Womenswear merchandiser Kathy Ferguson wore them to a sales conference; orders soared, and Lee had to order in more coloured thread to satisfy demand.
Left: Actress and singer Jane Birkin demonstrates the fashionable patched-denim look, 1971, in an out-take of the cover shoot for Serge Gainsbourg's album, Histoire De Melody Nelson.

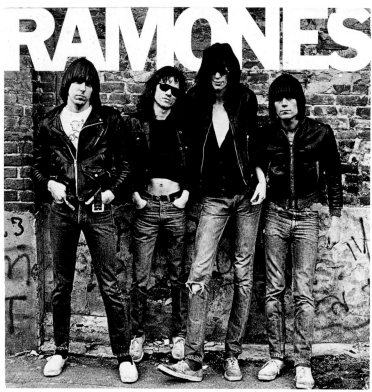

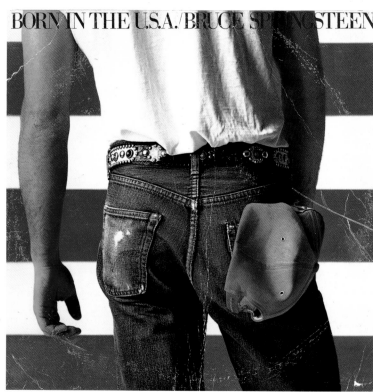

launch The Doors, and was a mainstay of Andy Warhol's Factory Scene. When he saw The Ramones play in a Bowery basement, he was overwhelmed by the dumb beauty of their music. He was equally struck by their style. "It was perfect; classic. What's better than jeans, a black leather jacket, and a white T-shirt? It's an easy and enduring look and costume that any kid in the world can create. It's the way you face the street. It's male, it's beautiful, it's tough and it doesn't date. Probably 50 years from now people will still be wearing black leather jackets and Levi's."

Denim dominates rock'n'roll cover art, in Neil Young's After The Goldrush (1970), the Stones' Warhol-designed Sticky Fingers (1971), Bruce Springsteen's Born In The USA (1984) and The Ramones' 1976 debut album. Later, denim was associated to its detriment with heavy rock (English metal fans play air guitar, circa 1984, right). Two decades later, patched flares and Metallica T-shirts would reach the high street!

Above: Mademoiselle cover, June 1942.
Denim is cut for a woman's curves with a higher waist, more tapered leg and sharp front creases. Lady Levi's, with pink selvage thread (instead of the usual red), were launched to cater for the increased demand for jeans by women. (Luis Kemus)

Left: Vogue, February 1938.
Denim continues to be presented as both functional and fashionable. Denim overalls set against a dramatic desert backdrop. (Tony Frissell)

Right: Vogue, May 1935
Western dress became fashionable following the popularity of Dude Ranches, where city women donned ranchers' clothing. Straight leg Levi's jeans turned up once at the hem. Cuban heel boots, plaid shirts and silk kerchiefs gave the ensemble an air of authenticity. Highland terrier optional. Vogue's feature marked the point at which Levi's jeans started to become known on the East Coast.

INDIGO GIRLS
From Lady Levi's to bumsters – denim is the fabric of fashion
by June Marsh

Denim has long been the fashion industry's right stuff. Over the years blue jeans have endured the harshest treatment: slashing, bleaching, ageing, shredding, tie dying, fraying and stonewashing. Yet denim has also been lavished with artistic embellishment: graffiti, beading, patchwork and embroidery, printing, covered with feathers and encrusted with crystals and diamonds. Designers have cut and re-engineered denim into every conceivable shape and form, and its continued appearance on the catwalk proves the

lucrative potential of this humble fabric. Undeniably cool and sexy, blue jeans continue to be the one item all women strive to squeeze into.

It was when western Dude Ranches sprouted as vacation spots for well-heeled city types that a new audience discovered the appeal of traditional jeanswear. Ranches in Nevada were especially popular, since Nevada was the state with the most relaxed divorce laws. Separated wives would spend two months at a ranch establishing residency, then leave joyfully with a divorce and a new fondness for denim. The Dude Ranch phenomenon led to the introduction in 1938 of Lady Levi's, "Designed with roomy hips and tapering trousers yet with all the rivets." Back in the city denim jeans became an original and impressive conversation piece and represented a new way to dress casually. In the summer of 1939 US Vogue endorsed denim by suggesting its busy readers should "Swop the traditional floral housecoat for denim overalls."

During the war years little was known in Europe of American designers, and although Valentina's classic gowns and Adrian's fabulous costumes for movie stars won some publicity, America still based her ready-to-wear trade on French fashions. It was not until the United States entered the war, when commercial relations between Paris couture houses and American buyers were severed, that native talent had its big opportunity. New York's World Fair in the summer of 1939 was instrumental in introducing American

Above left: Claire McCardell "Pop-over". Gouache sketch by McCardell of her original 1942 Pop-over dress, which sold in the hundreds of thousands. The Pop-over remained in McCardell's line in one form or another over the next 16 years. (Brooklyn Museum of Art Special Collections)

Above: Vogue, June 1952.
Lightweight denim day dress by Claire McCardell showing an infinitely feminine and remarkably modern design that helped launch her in the world of working women. Feminist Betty Friedman referred to McCardell in the late 1950s as "the girl who defied Dior". (Richard Rutledge)

Right: Vogue, April 1943.
In the 1940s Claire McCardell emerged as a powerful voice in dress design in America. Two thoroughly modern women show the new denim co-ordinates. A neat suit (right) and a lightweight denim, easy coat. (Horst)

designers whose ideas presented a more casual way for middle America to dress, replacing the formal niceties of pre-war life.

Claire McCardell was the young designer who played a crucial role in promoting contemporary American fashion, along with Tina Lester and Tom Brigance. McCardell is rightly credited with introducing "The American Look", in contrast to Dior's "New Look" of 1947. Born into a wealthy Southern family in a small town in Maryland, McCardell grew up with a great interest in fashion through her mother's imported Paris fashion magazines and a fascination for her brothers' clothes – which, by her early teens, she was dismantling and re-making for herself. The generous side pockets found in men's trousers particularly fascinated her, as did the deep armholes in men's jackets and Levi topstitching – crucial details which she would later incorporate into her design vocabulary. "I've always wondered why women's clothes had to be delicate," said McCardell. "Why couldn't they be practical and sturdy as well as feminine?"

McCardell graduated from what is now Parsons School Of Design in New York City, but while studying there went to Paris to observe the great dressmakers of the 1920s. Especially important for McCardell was Madeleine Vionnet, whose innovative construction and fabric-handling techniques, and intimately feminine designs, greatly influenced McCardell's own work.

As Kohle Yohannan and Nancy Nolf pointed out in their book, Claire McCardell: Redefining Modernism, "McCardell came of age when the whole country was shifting – not only had World War II imposed mass production restrictions but it brought women out of the home and into the workplace, where an affordable wardrobe was greatly needed."

Vogue, January 1968.
A mini, kimono-style dress in blue denim with an obi-style sash is worn by Countess Vera Von Lehndorff, known as Veruschka. One of the most famous models in magazine history, she was also one of the tallest at 6'1", and along with Princess Natasha Paley, one of the most aristocratic. (Franco Rubartelli)

Lady Levi's, Lot Number 701, were introduced around 1935 and soon became obligatory wear for female dude ranchers. This pair dates from the 1940s. (Heller's Café)

September 1969. Yves St Laurent flanked by two of his fashion models, Betty Calroux (left) and Lucie de la Falaise. St Laurent opened his own fashion house in 1962, and launched the first Rive Gauche boutiques in 1966. Here they are all wearing "jeans-influenced" outfits.

Newsweek, 1966: White Lee Westerners were the jeans of choice for English mods.

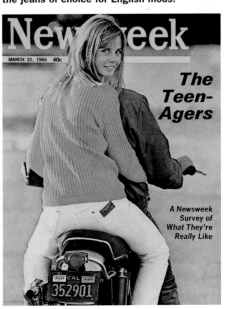

OCTOBER
House & Garden
SPECIAL FALL DECORATING ISSUE
75¢

NEW IDEAS FOR
BRINGING
ROOMS UP-TO-DATE

AN EXTRAORDINARY
NEW APARTMENT
BY BILLY BALDWIN

NEWS IN FURNITURE,
FABRICS, RUGS, ACCESSORIES
YOU CAN BUY RIGHT *NOW*

10 VARIATIONS ON
THE FAMILY-SIZED OMELETTE

LUSCIOUS SKILLET APPLES
AND WHISKEY APPLE PIE

15 THINGS TO COOK AHEAD
FOR CHRISTMAS

FRAGRANT CHOCOLATE
AND COFFEE DRINKS

House & Garden, 1973. Denim soft furnishings add a youthful element to a classic room set. (Horst)

The ubiquitous Wrangler flared jean

Looking for a slice of the action, Gloria Vanderbilt, the New York socialite turned designer, took the jeans phenomenon a notch higher by lending her upper class family name and ritzy glamour to Murjani's jeans brand.

McCardell nearly always disdained fancy fabrics in favour of calico, denim and the new stretch jerseys. During this time Diana Vreeland, then fashion editor of Harper's Bazaar, challenged McCardell, whose affordable and relaxed designs she personally admired, to create a stylish dress for busy housewives and mothers. The blue denim "Pop over", one of McCardell's most famous dresses, was given that name because you "just pop it over something nicer underneath." It was a simple, wrap-front denim dress, which even came with a matching oven glove and sold for just $6.95. This design was so copied that a patent was taken out by the designer, and in 1942 the Pop-over won McCardell a citation of honour from the panel of judges of the American Fashion Critics' Award. They acknowledged the design as "an outstanding interpretation of fashion trends under the restrictive influences of 1941".

By 1942 Vogue were showing "Victorettes", the provocatively named new work

Customized denim, floppy hats and skinny-rib sweaters were typically seen on weekend hippies, seen here parading through the mud at the Bardrey Pop Festival, Lincolnshire in 1972.

clothes for "women at war", including a short sleeved "coverall" and a jacket and slacks in faded blue denim. Wrangler and Lee launched their first jeans designed for women in 1949, and Claire McCardell continued to produce contemporary, affordable clothes for the new working woman. Her "comfort first" ideology was something she practised for more than 25 years and in her hands denim, for the first time, achieved an all important cachet among the fashionable cognoscenti of the East Coast. McCardell invented what we now call American sportswear; her designs were easy and modern, soft and elegant, including day and evening dresses, play clothes, suits and coats, and active sportswear.

As Levi's sales soared to 100 million pairs a year in the 1960s, the French couture heads sent out a committee to study the new production methods and returned greatly impressed. Denim had become a badge of social ethics and group identity – an anti-fashion fashion. And while the international ready-to-wear market still seemed obsessed

Calvin Klein Jeans

by Paris couture, the mood of fashion was rapidly changing. Many of the younger Paris couturiers were being influenced by the art-school trained British designers who were making London the fashion capital of the world. Many of the most influential British designers were women – Mary Quant, Zandra Rhodes, Barbara Hulanicki, Jean Muir and Thea Porter. Ossie Clarke was the most innovative young male designer, working successfully with Celia Birtwell's fabulous prints. It was a time of romance and fantasy, as well as the classless society. Catherine Deneuve married David Bailey, arriving at the church smoking, Bailey dressed casually in sweater and corduroy jeans; the best man, Mick Jagger, wore a blue denim suit. There were no longer dress codes – everyone did their own thing. Ethnic ideas were introduced, often mixed or made entirely of denim or chambray. Psychedelic prints as panels, appliqués and patches customized otherwise plain denim clothes.

In Paris, Yves Saint Laurent, who was particularly fond of denim and had the knack of transforming everyday clothes into ingeniously elegant designs, began to use denim in his ready-to-wear collections, as if it were something much more luxurious, such as cashmere or silk. His first recorded use of denim was in 1969 – "a dramatic, swirling redingote with matching boots" – and later, in the 1970s, the denim trouser suits in his collections were an absolute must for any fashion conscious woman.

Denim was well established in the youth market by the end of the 1960s and innovative new jeans brands began to emerge. One of the earliest in the UK to have a high fashion profile was South Sea Bubble. Set up in Kensington Market in London by Charles Hirsch, it was best remembered for bleached, brushed denim "loons", which had low, narrow waistbands, tight upper legs and were flared from the knee. Brushed denim gave the appearance of being well worn; this brand was also influential in the use of coloured brushed denim.

The 1970s were the golden age for denim: dungarees, bib and brace, bell bottoms and flares. Turned up cuffs on straight cuts were de rigueur and there was denim in

KATHARINE HAMNETT
DENIM

Katharine Hamnett revived denim in the summer of 1984 just as many fashion commentators were ready to write off blue jeans. Hamnett presented the industry with new challenges, including "shredded" denim. A new wave of textured denim treatments followed and the "hard times" trend was launched.

THE DENIM EDGE

It's clear right off—there's a different approach to denim today. Now, it's taken on a definite edge—in strong daytime dressing, straightforward "real-life" clothes—with far more design than the "gear" ever had. The best—on these four pages. Thierry Mugler's two-piece charcoal denim dress, this page. Its emphatically body-conscious shape—the curved skirt; the big-shouldered jacket, held at the waist—gives it distinctive appeal. Jacket and skirt, about $900. Bloomingdale's; Lou Lattimore, Dallas. . . . Also, opposite: Azzedine Alaïa's denim jacket. . .very much the sculptured signature Alaïa shape: it's full-sleeved, zippered, holds its own over his opalescent mini-dress. Cotton jacket, about $455. Cotton/viscose dress, about $210. Barneys New York; Colili, Millburn NJ; Linda Dresner, Troy MI; Ultimo, Chicago; Alaïa Chez Galley, Beverly Hills. Hair, these four pages, Julien for Is, Paris; makeup, Stephan Marais. For details, more stores, see last pages of this issue.

Steven Meisel

Vogue, April 1986. This magazine spread of photos by Steven Meisel proves the power of design manipulation by two brilliant fashion designers. A denim two-piece by Thierry Mugler (left) and from the "King of Cling" Azzedine Alaia, a denim jacket in his sculptured signature Alaia shape – full-sleeved, zippered – holding its own over his opalescent mini dress.

stonewashed and hardcore finishes. Cheap Chic was essential reading; the American style bible, written by Catherine Milinaire and Carol Troy, it walked off the shelves and is today highly sought after by fashion collectors. They wrote, "In the basics, sic blue jeans, you can remain anonymous, observe and stalk the life you're after on a quiet and individual style." That snippet of advice seems ironic now considering the choice of cover girl – the yet-to-be-discovered Jerry Hall.

Denim became glamorous in the 1970s – a blank canvas to be painted, embroidered, studded, patched and fringed. Rock stars began applying glitter and fashion styling to basic denim and people started experimenting with the classic cuts. You were judged by the width of your flares, and the label on your back pocket became the all-important badge of hipness. Designers cut denim into skirts, dresses, jackets and overalls, as well as blue jeans. Real life denim became "life-style" denim. In 1971 denim was officially made respectable. The Coty Fashion Critics Award for world fashion influence – the Seventh Avenue Oscar – was awarded to Levi Strauss.

Although it was Calvin Klein who created America's first pair of designer jeans in 1977, Gloria Vanderbilt was quick to follow the trend, taking the phenomenon a notch higher in 1978 by lending her upper-class family name and ritzy glamour to blue denim jeans. Vanderbilt popularized designer jeans for a wider class of American women who wanted comfort and durability rather than the more expensive and tighter fit jeans popular in Europe. Her signature line and stretch jeans were produced by Murgani USA.

Sharon Stone wears Gap deconstructed jeans jacket and fishnets. Since its beginnings in 1969, Gap has provided modern classic clothing for all the family.

Denim jeans were now a high status garment; from Rodeo Drive to St Tropez, other big name designers followed: Ralph Lauren, Diane von Fürstenberg, Fiorucci, Armani. Denim became a way to polish up an image and did not stop at clothing alone. In fact, as far back as 1973 the Wolfsburg Volkswagen company decided to spruce up the ageing VW Beetle. The marque 34h8 VW1200 was offered in a special yellow version with side and rear sticker strips saying "Jeans Bug". The seat covers were made of denim with coloured saddle stitch seams and rivets.

Launched in 1991, the Versace Jeans Couture line was an instant success, and although expensive it soon became the leading jeans label in the top women's market segment. The designs reflected Versace's creativity with their sleek, body-conscious fit and innovative fabrics featuring bright colours, bold graphics and typical Versace patterns. Modelled by the "Supers", Linda Evangelista, Stephanie Seymour and Christy Turlington.

Always on Camera, 1992. From Vivienne Westwood's autumn/winter 1992/3 ready-to-wear collection, a mid-calf length skirt showing the face of Marlene Dietrich. From the collection of Stephen Philip at Relik. (Geoff Dann)

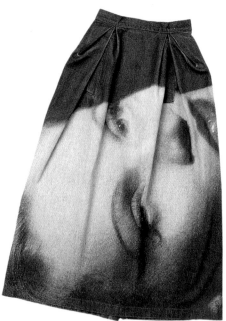

While Vanderbilt was selling jeans through glamour, Calvin Klein was already well known for his provocative advertising campaigns. His most daring promotion came in 1980 when he cast 15-year-old Brooke Shields to star in his TV and press advertisements. She tossed her hair, spread her long legs wide and declared, "Between me and my Calvin's there is absolutely nothing." Shields also confessed she had "seven Calvins in my closet – if they could talk I would be ruined." Middle America was more than a little shocked, and several local TV stations pulled the ads. Klein defiantly continued to quote "Jeans are Sex." Of course, that did not prevent Shields from earning between $400,000 and $1 million, and Klein's sales leaping to $180 million from a mere

Savagely elegant ensemble by Jean Paul Gaultier from his 1994 "Pierced and Tattooed" ready-to-wear collection. The dramatic crinoline skirt made from a patchwork of used denim is worn with a white frock coat and blue beads. The heavy boots and nose chain are obvious reminders of the rebellious mood of both denim and this designer. Illustration by Gladys Perint Palmer

Vivienne Westwood, from the summer 1991 collection entitled "Cut, Slash and Pull". A provocative collection of jeans wear texturized by cutting, slashing and shredding the denim. (Chris Moore)

$25 million the previous year.

Designer jeans took a hold in Europe in the early 1980s, symbolizing a return to affluence. Knife-edge creases, mixed with Lycra, tamed with luxurious fabrics like silk and cashmere, linen and fur all added status to the basic denim jean. Denim was worn in the office with twin-set and pearls or at Harry's Bar with black tie and diamonds. Every designer from Karl Lagerfeld at Chanel to "King of Cling" Azzedine Alaïa included denim in their collections.

Denim was now a high status, high priced cloth, and, for all its gloss and glamour, was at risk of losing its lucrative youth market as sales of the traditional brands fell. People

no longer wanted to buy a uniform; instead they wanted to look elegant. Perhaps that was why Levi Strauss & Co. commissioned Saint Martin's School of Art first- and second-year MA Students to focus their imagination on classic denim fashion garments. Most students rejected the then naff stonewashed or any other kind of bastardized denim, and went for unwashed indigo. The first prize went to Lloyd Cracknell, who teamed classic Levi 501s with a funky new coat and blouse design, more or less indicating the way denim jeans were heading – right back to type.

The mid-1980s economic recession hit the jeans market badly and many fashion commentators were ready to write denim's obituary. But it was not to be. During the

From US designer Marc Jacob's casual yet luxurious take on blue jeans to fashionista's favourite, Roberto Cavalli, there is a designer jean to suit everybody. Clockwise from top left: Marc Jacobs, 1991; Alexander McQueen's infamous "bumsters", 2000; Roberto Cavalli, 2001; leg'o'mutton sleeve jacket, Dolce & Gabbana, 2001; couture ballgown by Jean Paul Gaultier, 1999.

summer of 1984 Katharine Hamnett made her name by putting anti-missile messages on T-shirts and later that year produced a new collection including "shredded" denim jeans; thus the "hard times" look was born.

Vivienne Westwood followed with a spring/summer 1991 collection entitled "Cut, Slash and Pull", featuring sexy denim styles textured by cutting, slashing and shredding the fabric. Westwood continued the denim theme with the "Always on Camera" collection, depicting over-sized, printed photographic images of Hollywood legends such as Marlene Dietrich on contemporary denim pieces.

In Europe, Jean Paul Gaultier and Yves Saint Laurent recognized the power and

Tom Ford's pocahontas-style jeans for Gucci carried an outrageously high price tag (£2000/$3000), yet they were an instant sell-out. Top designers are still madly, deeply, in love with denim. Clockwise from top left: Dior, 2000; Chanel, 2000; Gucci, 1999; Fake London, 2001; Dolce & Gabbana, 2001. All photographs by Chris Moore

influence of street-fashion early in their careers, and have both contributed greatly to jeans culture. Among Gaultier's early innovations were the plastic jeans jacket and the bad-boy jean with lace-up back (itself an echo of traditional designs by companies like Carhartt) and, later, more extravagant designs like the enormous, billowing patchwork skirts (1994) and shredded denim, strapless ballgown for his haute couture collection in 1999.

Versace Jeans Couture was launched in 1991 and, though expensive, soon became the leading jeans label in the top women's market segment. The cut was sleek and body-conscious, innovative fabrics including bright colours and bold pattern – it was typically exhibitionist.

The Earl Jean brand was hatched in LA by Suzanne Costas Friewald and Ben Friewald, and has since grown into a multimillion-dollar company. Suzanne, the designer, had, like Claire McCardell, been altering the cut of jeans for years for herself and her friends – typically starting with men's jeans, preferring the lower cut, removing the waistband, cutting them down to make them lower still, slimming the leg to pencil-thin and leaving a light boot-cut at the bottom. What emerged was the Earl style 55: the original Earl low-waist jean. Since then the line has broadened significantly, and no snake-hipped female celebrity can live without a pair of Earls, typically worn with either Manolo Blahnik or Jimmy Choo spike high heels.

Helmut Lang launched his revelatory dark denim and further enhanced his cool design reputation. Gucci's Pocahontas jeans launched in 1999 (at £2,000 a pair) and were the hottest sample in the Gucci press cupboard. Marc Jacobs' and Daryl K's denim ranges also proved much sought-after by the fashion cognoscenti.

By the end of the 1990s dark, tight original Calvins, vintage Gloria's and low waist, long-legged Earls were familiar sights among the fashion and celebrity crowd. Denim jeans now turn up consistently in the front row of fashion shows and at the after show parties. A thousand paparazzi pictures appeared of Kate Moss in jeans, skimpy little tops and high heels, which soon turned into a mainstream trend; equally, the iconic jeans jacket still remains an all-time favourite.

Blue jeans have undeniably lost none of their enduring sex appeal. At Alexander McQueen, famous for his bumster jeans, a separate jeans line was launched in July 2000. Now jeans hang alongside the rest of the range: "I don't see the jeans as a diffusion range," McQueen says arrogantly. "They're designed in the same way as the main collection; if you're aware that you are making something cheap, you are never going to come up with the new 501." Joining the ranks of jeans genies is Stella McCartney, who has gathered a predictably star-studded following for her seductive line in denim.

As I write, there are bound to be new denim brands ready for the limelight, they could be John Galliano's funky dark denim piped with leather for Dior; Chanel's blue-black dirty denim; West Coast style-leaders Juicy Couture's low-cut, "ultra-sassy" flares, or Earl Jean's new straight-fit jeans. Then there's 2 Jeans from Katayone Adeli, the New York designer whose trousers are considered the most flattering in the world. Whatever happens next in fashion, you can be sure denim is here to stay – enjoy that comforting thought!

Material girl: Madonna, 2000, photographed by Jean-Baptiste Mondino. Madonna chose cowboy blues from Dolce & Gabbana for her Music album.

DESIGNER DENIM
At the end of the catwalk shows, designers of both sexes take a bow in – what else – denim!

Jean Paul Gaultier   Alexander McQueen   Rifat Ozbek

Marc Jacobs   Tom Ford   Ralph Lauren

Stella McCartney

Dolce & Gabbana

John Galliano

Michael Kors

Calvin Klein

Giorgio Armani

Levi's legendary Launderette commercial of 1986, featuring model Nick Kamen stripping to his boxer shorts, accompanied by a Marvin Gaye soundalike. Made by UK agency Bartle, Bogle, Hegarty, the commercial put Marvin Gaye back in the Top 10 singles chart, inspired Kamen to embark on a short-lived singing career and helped make Levi's 501 the most popular jeans on the planet. Levi's huge success in the US and Europe would eventually cause problems, when their jeans became too ubiquitous to be fashionable.

IT'S THE CAT'S WHISKERS
Jeans get stonewashed, sandpapered – and distressed

By the early 1980s, consumers wanted something entirely new. The 1960s were a distant memory, flared jeans an embarrassing anachronism. It was time for a radical innovation. Namely, 1950s nostalgia.

Levi Strauss & Co. had seen off many competitors via intensive advertising from its very earliest days. That tradition continued when the 1986 European advertising campaign for 501 jeans, produced by London agency Bartle, Bogle, Hegarty, was one of the most successful campaigns in the history of advertising. But even as the Levi's commercials hit the screen, a part of the heritage they depicted was disappearing forever. In 1983 Cone Mills, which made the denim for the 501, switched from 29-inch looms to more efficient 58-inch machines, causing the disappearance of the distinctive selvage stripe, which had already gone from LS&Co.'s European-sourced jeans. By 1985, European dealers were selling used and "dead-stock" American 501s, and the term "selvage" passed into general use as collectors looked for the distinctive red line – akamini, to the Japanese – that marked a pair of vintage Levi's. It was hardly surprising that over the same period a few smaller concerns started exploring the concept of replicating vintage jeans. Adriano Goldschmied, a founder of the Genius Group who is regarded by many as the industry's foremost vintage denim expert, started to make his

Custom car rally on London's King's Road in the late 1980s. Levi's emphasis on the 501 jean dovetailed perfectly with a UK and US rockabilly revival; for half a decade the 501 would be a staple of street style *and* the high street.

Evis Model 1500 jacket, 1990; an instant hit with fashionistas, it was one of the products that would help the renamed Evisu become a leader in vintage-look, dark denim. The jacket was influenced by Levi's originals, but was not a direct copy. The painted arcuate, however, was very close to Levi's wartime painted design, while the red tab is essentially that of "Big E" Levi's, with the initial L removed. Around this time, UK Evis retailers were forced to cut off the red Evis tab by pressure from Levi's distributors.

Evis not only produced faithful replicas of Lee's 101Z and 101J denim; it also fashioned its own outfit for Lee's Buddy Lee doll. The mini Evis overalls are fitted to an original pre-1950s Buddy Lee composition doll. (Dispensary For Kids)

name around 1983 with Goldie's Oldies – jeans featuring printed-on "cat's whiskers" (the distinctive wear pattern around the crotch) and sandblasted knees.

Throughout the 1970s and 1980s, the major manufacturers were churning out pale denim that was generally pre-washed or stonewashed. More and more jeans were being produced with open-end yarn, a faster and cheaper method of processing cotton that produced bulkier, fluffier denim. Modern jeans bore less and less resemblance to the vintage article.

By the late 1980s, Japan was becoming the world's foremost consumer of vintage denim. Fortuitously, it was also the home of some of the world's finest small fabric mills, most notably Kurabo and Nisshinbo, both based in Osaka, and Hiroshima's Kaihara. Each of them produced high-quality, ring-spun denim in the old-fashioned 29-inch width. Soon companies like Evis and Edwin were using this denim to make lovingly-crafted vintage style jeans, in the process inspiring the apocryphal story that Levi Strauss & Co. had sold off their looms to Evis or other Japanese manufacturers. In fact, Cone Mills, who made the denim for Levi's jeans, had simply put their old 29-inch looms in the basement; as demand for vintage-style fabric boomed, they would later dust them off and put them back into service.

As the big American jeans manufacturers concentrated on the mass market, Japanese and European designers found themselves on the cutting edge of the high street. Adriano Goldschmied founded the Genius Group in the late 1970s; it would become a hugely influential conglomerate, the source of many labels, including Diesel, Replay, Martin Guy

and Katherine Hamnett. Goldschmied left the group in 1985 but continued his quest to replicate the look and feel of worn-in, vintage Levi's: "I became interested in vintage jeans in the very early '80s. In the late '70s the cut and the design defined jeans. Then finishing became crucial; in thinking about the finishing we changed the design concept of jeans and then we started to think of the vintage jean as an inspiration point. But it was a slow, laborious journey!"

Goldschmied soon moved on from printed-on cat's whiskers, working closely with the Martelli laundry, based in Bologna, Italy. By the mid-1980s they had developed pioneering new techniques to distress jeans and replicate specific wear such as "cat's whiskers" using a system of abrasive brushes. Goldschmied's Rivet range is often cited as the first modern jeans to combine authentic selvage fabric, from Kurabo, with convincing replication of wear and cat's whiskers. The influence of Goldschmied and Martelli's work can be seen today on countless high streets.

Diesel's Old Glory collection, launched in 1991, was a clear sign of where the jeans market was heading. Designed by Wilbert Das, Marly Nijssen, Renny Blasselle and Olivier Reboul, the collection comprised vintage-influenced jeans and jackets in various fabrics, including denim from Kurabo, Kaihara and the Italian company Legler. There was a purist feel to the Old Glory range, which included denim in a right-hand twill, just like Levi's; a softer left-hand twill, like Lee; and a broken twill, like Wrangler. By Diesel's standards the jeans were expensive, but as Marly Nijssen points out, "Diesel wanted to show the world we knew how to produce jeans: we were very precise in the construction, with

Press advertisement for Diesel's Old Glory range, 1991. Diesel's founder Renzo Rosso is shown bottom right. The Old Glory range signalled Diesel's ascendance in the denim high-street market, giving the brand a cachet that eluded established names like Levi's and Lee in the 1990s.

internal rivets, open seams, extremely precise detailing. And they were never reproduction, they were always with a twist." The range featured embroideries, "repairs" and cat's whiskers – all courtesy of Martelli. Old Glory was the flagship product that signalled Diesel's upcoming dominance of the European jeans market – several of the designs and finishes remained in the company's mass-market range ten years later. Another Genius group company, Replay, also concentrated on the look and feel of vintage denim; although its jeans didn't copy cosmetic details, the finish and "wear" of many of its "double-ring spun" jeans was uncannily reminiscent of vintage Levi's.

The late 1990s, and dark denim rules. This page, clockwise from top left: Flying F stretch jeans, Silas, Anglomania by Vivienne Westwood, Evisu embroidered logo, Calvin Klein, Eley Tishomoto. Opposite page, clockwise from top left: Carhartt workpants, Lois Cherry N2, G Star Elwood jeans, Lee Riders.

Ironically, as more companies attempted to replicate the feel of early Levi's jeans, Levi Strauss & Co. seemed oblivious of its own heritage. Although LS&Co. Japan enjoyed success with its reissue range, which commenced with 1987's 502 replica made of Kurabo denim, a new generation of purists turned to companies like Evis, who produced lovingly-crafted vintage style jeans in stiff, dark denim, much of it, according to insiders, sourced from Kurabo. Evis jeans started making their name outside of Japan in 1989; by 1990 the company was making a huge range of vintage copies, including versions of Lee 101 jeans and jackets (complete with a painted version of Lee's 'Lazy S' logo), various

Left: 2002, and nouveau New York new wavers The Strokes champion the return of ripped, skinny-leg jeans and Converse high tops, à la Ramones.

Below: The Wrangler brand enjoys its own style revival thanks to diminutive Oz singer Kylie Minogue, who also wears vintage Levi's 501s... and not much else.

bib overalls, and Levi's 557 jacket. However, its most popular lines evoked the general look of 1930s or 1940s Levi's, without being specific copies. Although Evis's founder, Hidehiko Yamame, was forced to change the name of his jeans to Evisu, thanks to legal threats from Levi Strauss & Co., he enjoyed the consolation of seeing his own jeans become one of the most popular premium brands.

Although LS&Co. enjoyed its most successful year ever in 1990, commanding 31% of the US jeans market, it would soon be squeezed in every conceivable direction. Store-owned labels like JC Penney's Arizona brand challenged in lower price ranges; Tommy Hilfiger and DKNY (designed by Goldschmied's Team Kit), once seen as designer labels, became mass-market brands. By the mid-1990s, San Francisco retailer Gap had opened stores worldwide and soon presented a serious threat to Levi's jeans with products such as the 1969 range – designed by, once again, Adriano Goldschmied's Team Kit.

At a time when LS&Co.'s heritage seemed a burden, venerable rivals such as Ben Davis and Carhartt prospered as hip hop acts started dressing in dark denim workwear worn baggy and low-slung – legendarily to replicate the style of convicts forced to hand in their belts. The Ben Davis company was founded by the grandson of Jacob Davis, Levi Strauss's one-time business partner, in 1935. Their baggy workshirts, initially based on

Boss of the Road patterns, became de rigueur thanks to the patronage of West Coast acts like Dr. Dre – who opens his wardrobe in one video to reveal 20 identical black Ben Davis shirts. Newer labels followed, such as FUBU – founded in 1992 by Daymond John in Hollis, Queens – and Rocawear, part-owned by rapper Jay-Z. LS&Co. languished in comparison and was forced to rethink its jeans from first principles: "It was around 1993 that we were starting to lose our credibility with opinion-formers," admits Peter Ingwersen, European brand director of LS&Co.'s premium products. "It took us a couple of years to react to that problem and do something about it."

In 1998 Ingwersen was charged with solving the company's image problem. Concentrating initially on moving up-market, LS&Co. Europe co-ordinated a new international vintage reissue programme and introduced a new premium range: Red. London-based designer Rikke Korff took a problem that had long afflicted vintage Levi's – the leg twist – and used it in exaggerated form for a pair of Red jeans in 1999. The following spring the new Engineered range, complete with twisted seams, hit the high street. Baggy, low-slung, often in a single-back-pocket configuration that harked back to Levi's jeans of 1873, the Engineered range helped resuscitate Levi's reputation in Europe. The most sincere testament to their success came from rival manufacturers,

Top: Rapper LL Cool J models for FUBU. Above, FUBU's metallic denim shirt epitomizes the shiny denim look popular in rap circles. FUBU is part of a new generation of influential labels in which a rap connection seems obligatory: Rocawear is part-owned by Jay-Z, Phat Farm is co-owned by Def Jam founder Russell Simmons, while P Diddy and J-Lo's own labels are already proven money-spinners.

Above: Lee Europe's reissue of the company's classic 101Z zipper jeans. Lee Europe and Lee's Japanese licensee, Edwin, have both produced finely-crafted reissues, sold through small outlets. The European 101Z reissue, with selvage fabric, first appeared in 1992, laying the foundation for the company's successful 101 and Denim 42 range, launched in 2001.

Left: Classic, with a twist – Levi's Engineered range, which helped re-establish Levi's reputation in Europe. Below: where it all began: Levi's 2001 replica of the 1880s jeans pictured on page 10. The natural indigo denim comes from Kurabo, Osaka; the wear and patches are courtesy of the Bart Sights laundry, Kentucky.

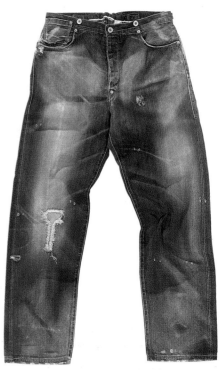

including London's fcuk, France's Teddy Smith and Japan's Michiko Koshino, who introduced dark, baggy jeans with twisted seams. Poignantly, when LS&Co. purchased the earliest-known pair of Levi's in 2001, for $45,000, these venerable jeans perfectly exemplified the current look: baggy workwear cut, accessory pocket (perhaps designed for a pair of pliers, but just as suited to a mobile phone or MP3 player) and heavily distressed finish. Appropriately enough, they inspired a painstakingly accurate reissue.

The first Levi's jeans soon found themselves the subject of cut-throat commercial competition. Well over a century later, that competition is more cut-throat still, as old rivals like Lee undergo a renaissance, and recent interlopers such as Diesel, Evisu, Earl and Juicy Couture join up-market rivals like Dolce & Gabbana, Gucci and Versace. As far as most designers are concerned, the magic of denim will never fade. The biggest problem most of them contend with is that there's simply not enough being produced.

No other fabric is as easy to work with – or as unknowable. As Adriano Goldschmied crystallizes it, "Denim has a life of its own. It changes with the body – and develops a long-lasting personal attachment to its wearer." So, it is an anthropomorphic fabric. And it loves us, too.

GLOSSARY

Amoskeag

A New Hampshire factory town which was the first major source of denim in the US. The Amoskeag Manufacturing Company opened in 1838 and by 1900 claimed to be the world's biggest textile producer; it later declined due to industrial unrest and competition from southern mills. Amoskeag denim was used exclusively for Levi's 501 until 1915.

Arcuate

Distinctive double stitching used on the back pocket of the very first Levi's jeans, now acknowledged as the world's oldest clothing trademark. Early examples, all hand-stitched, can differ considerably in shape. The shape became synonymous with Levi's jeans by 1900, although it's conceivable that other early workwear might have used the device before them. LS&Co. trademarked the stitching in 1943.

Back cinch

Also known as a martingale, the back cinch with a back buckle was used to tighten the waist on jeans before widespread use of belts; hence the term "buckle back". Most jeans makers abandoned them by 1942; with renewed interest in vintage-style looks, cinchbacks have returned on modern jeans including Evisu, Levi's Engineered and G Star.

Big-E

A term used to describe Levi's clothing made before 1971, at which time the all upper-case logo on the red tab was redesigned with a lower case E.

Broken Twill

A denim weave, invented by John Neil Walker, which changes direction in order to prevent leg twist (see photo, right). This weave was used by Wrangler from 1965 for its 13MWZ jeans, and by 1980s designer brands like Jordache and Calvin Klein. This twill is easy to spot; look inside a Wrangler jacket to see the zig-zag weave pattern.

Clarkson, Jeremy

This Levi's-clad UK TV presenter, usually seen in a lascivious clinch with a souped-up hatchback, was the inspiration behind the term "Jeremy Clarkson effect"; namely, the off-putting aesthetic effect of a middle-aged male crammed into a skin-tight pair of Levi's. Insiders in the denim industry claim such horrors were the reason Levi Strauss & Co. was forced to update its image with the Engineered range.

Cone Mills

Cone Mills started producing denim in 1895 in Greensboro, North Carolina. The company started supplying denim for Levi's jeans in 1910, becoming the exclusive supplier for the 501 in 1922. Cone is still one of the world's biggest denim manufacturers.

Denim

Denim is an indigo-dyed cotton twill fabric, woven with a dyed warp yarn and a natural fill yarn. The term derives from Serge De Nimes; but denim and Serge De Nimes are different fabrics.

Indigo

The dye used for denim, initially taken from the *indigofera tinctoria* plant. It was synthesized 14 years after its chemical structure was identified by Adolf Bayer in 1897. Pre-1920s jean were generally dyed with natural indigo and were – as far as one can tell by comparing vintage examples – paler in colour, with a green cast. Later jeans were a darker blue, particularly used in combination with sulphur dyes (see *Sulphur Bottom*).

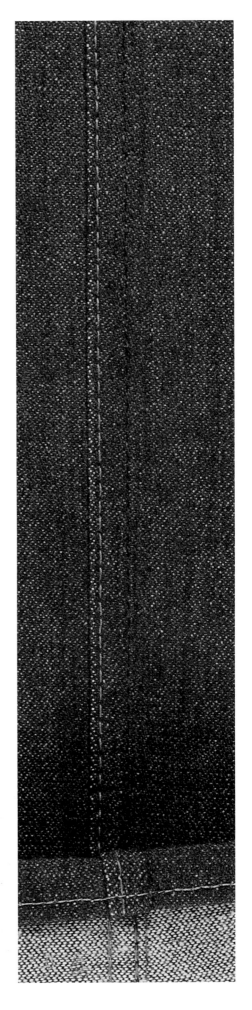

Laundry

Laundries are companies that "finish" jeans, washing them or distressing them for a worn-in look. Most major jeans manufacturers use several different laundries which specialize in different finishes. The main techniques include simple washing, stonewashing, use of a "Tonello" machine with abrasive bristles, sandblasting or applying enzymes to simulate "cat's whisker" wear lines – and sandpapering by hand!

Left-hand twill

See *Right-hand twill* for explanation. Left-hand twill was traditionally used on Lee jeans (see photo, right), but its "softer" feel is becoming more and more popular and is now used on Levi's Silver Tab range and Calvin Klein jeans.

Leg twist

Many vintage jeans suffer from leg twist. This is simply a natural adjustment of the fabric, which tends to follow the direction of the weave. Stefano Aldighieri, Director of Fabric & Finishing, at LS&Co. explains it thus: "Levi's denim were mostly right-hand twills; the twill line rises to the right. During the weaving process you basically 'force' the fabric to be straight, perpendicular to the selvage, but at the same time you give it this direction in the construction. You lay and cut the fabric; in the early days LS&Co. patterns were cut straight along the selvage. When you wash the garments, the fabric will try to follow the direction of the weave and will pull in that direction... hence the twisted legs, the result of the movement of the fabric. Because Lee started to use left-hand weave denims, their legs would twist the other way." Leg twist was eliminated in the 1970s by skewing (which contorts denim to its after-wash shape) – and later revived with Levi's Red and Engineered twisted seams jeans!

Open End denim

Open End or OE spinning was introduced in the 1970s, reducing costs by omitting several elements of the traditional spinning process. The cotton fibres are 'mock twisted' by blowing them together. Open End denim is bulkier, coarser and darker, because it absorbs more dye, and wears less well than *Ring Spun* denim. Although cheaper to produce it has been used on many designer jeans, including Calvin Klein and Tommy Hilfiger.

Right-hand twill

Most denim is right-hand twill, a weave which produces a diagonal, or twill, line which rises from left to right. This was standard practice in weaving; single yarn warps were woven right-hand, double yarn warps were woven left hand. Most Levi's jeans are right-hand twill (see photo, far right); many Lee jeans are left-hand twill.

Ring-Spun denim

Ring-Spun yarns were traditionally used in denim up until the late 1970s, but were later supplanted by cheaper *Open End* yarns. The term has become used more in recent years, as a vintage look becomes more prized; Claudio Buziol of the Italian Replay company was probably the first purist to use the term on his vintage-style product. Ring-Spun fibres are twisted together – as opposed to merely blown together, as in Open End yarns – and are consequently stronger; they look less '"fluffy" than Open End denim, are harder-wearing and give a more desirable vintage look.

Ring/Ring denim

Ring/Ring, or Double Ring-Spun denim uses *Ring-Spun* yarn for both warp and weft. This is the traditional way to produce denim. It's possible to combine a ring-spun warp fabric

with an Open End weft, to get much of the strength and look of the traditional Ring/Ring denim at lower cost. Gap's Best Basics jeans used Ring/Open End denim supplied by Cone Mills.

Sanforization

A process which shrinks and stabilizes cloth before it is cut, Sanforization was invented by Sanford L. Cluett, of Cluett, Peabody and Co. with Jared C. Fox of the Globe Corporation. Patented in 1928, the process was reportedly first used by Erwin Mills in 1936 to make denim for overalls marketed under JC Penney's Big Mac label. Lee jeans were made from Sanforized fabric soon afterwards; Lady Levi's, introduced around 1935, were also Sanforized, although most other Levi's jeans remained shrink-to-fit for another three decades.

Selvage

Selvage is the narrow, white woven edge of vintage-style denim. It prevents unravelling of the denim, and has become synonymous with vintage jeans because it signals the use of narrow 29-inch looms, which were mothballed around 1983 by companies like Cone Mills in favour of more efficient 58 to 62-inch looms. Selvage usually boasts a white edge and often a coloured line which was added by the mills to identify their customers' fabric – red for most vintage Levi's from 1927, pink for Lady Levi's, plain white or green for most Lee jeans and gold for some Wrangler and JC Penney jeans.

Stonewashing

Reputedly invented by Hollywood Western Wear consultant Nudie Cohen around 1960, the stonewashing process distresses jeans by washing them along with pumice stones, which abrade the fabric and give it a worn-in look. Commercially, the process was pioneered by the French couple Marithé and François Girbaud, and was first used by the CA label in 1965. Its first large-scale use was by Lee jeans in 1982. Stonewashing is time-consuming; many laundries now achieve similar finishes using enzymes.

Sulphur Bottom

Many manufacturers apply a sulphur dye before the customary indigo dye; this is known as Sulphur Bottom dying. This can be used to create a grey or yellow "vintage" cast.

Waist Overalls

The original term for what we now know as jeans; Levi's continued to use this term up until the 1960s, to distinguish their jeans from bib overalls.

Warp

Yarn that runs parallel to the selvage; in denim it's dyed indigo.

Weft

Weft, or Filling Yarn, runs from selvage to selvage at right angles to the warp yarn; in denim, this yarn is left a natural, un-dyed colour.

Weight

Denim is traditionally graded by its weight per yard of fabric at a 29-inch width. Early Levi's were 9oz denim, increasing to 10oz in 1927; Lee 101 Cowboy Pants were introduced in the much heavier 13oz weight; most modern jeans are around 14oz.

Yoke

V-shaped section at the back of jeans, also known as a "riser", which gives curve to the seat. The deeper the V of the yoke, the greater the curve. Cowboy jeans often feature a deep yoke; workwear or dungaree jeans might have a shallower yoke – or no yoke at all.

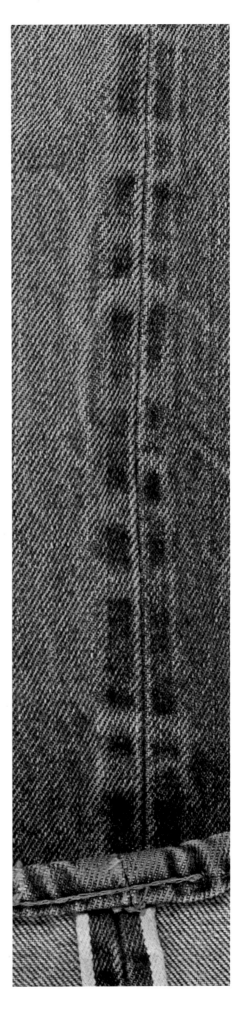

INDEX

PHOTOGRAPHIC CREDITS

Advertising Archives 104 (x2), 102 (Vanderbilt ad), 106 (Versace), 114, 117; Dennis Alstrand 71; Amoskeag Historical Society 17 (bottom right); Arizona Historical Society 50; Carolyn Cassady 80; Giancarlo Botti/Camerapress 93; Corbis 5, 21; Dorothea Lange/Corbis 25, 126; Arthur Rothstein/Corbis 57; Norman Rockwell/Curtis Publishing 61; Matthew Donahue 69 (main pic); Ray Burniston/EMI Records 120; Fubu 121 (x2); Arnold Newman/Getty Images 81; Tommy Hanley 91; Hulton Archive 36, 42, 68, 74, 103; Indigo 35, 116 (x2), 118 (all pics), 122 (top right), 123, 124, 125; Indigo/Babcock 9 (x2), 17 (top right), 18 (right), 20 (top left and right), 22 (right), 23 (x2), 44 (x2), 48 (bottom centre), 72 (x2), 76, 84 (right), 90 (bottom right); Keystone 83 (Joseph Beuys); Kobal Collection 41, 77 (x2), 89; Lee Archives 24,26 (main pic & top right), 27 (all pics), 28 (x2), 29, 30, 31 (x2), 32 (x4), 33, 34, 38, 39, 43, 45 (x4), 47 (x3), 48 (top and bottom ; left), 52 (x4), 53, 54 (x3), 55, 58 (x2), 62 (main ad), 63 (x3), 74 (Ads), 93 (right), 128; LS & Co Archives 6 (x3), 7, 8, 11, 12, 13, 14, 15 (x2), 16, 17(left), 18 (left), 19 (x2), 20(bottom left), 22 (top and bottom left), 37 (x3), 42 (bottom), 48 (bottom right), 49, 56 (x3), 60 (x2), 62 (top right x2), 66, 84 (left), 122 (top left, bottom right); Nicolas Schul/LS & Co 10; Eve Arnold/Magnum 3, 78; Bruce Davidson/Magnum 82; Danny Lyon/Magnum 83 (Dylan); Dennis Stock/Magnum 75 (Warhol); Inge Morath/Magnum 72; Lee Miller Archives 82 (Picasso and Max Ernst); National Archives 59, 69 (bottom right); Sunday Times/News International 82 (Peter Blake); PA Photos 113 (top left); JC Penney 24; Pictorial 1, 40, 64 (wrangler ad), 79; Ted Polhemus/PYMCA 115; David Redfern/Redferns 90; Elliott Landy/Redferns 88; Michael Ochs Archives/Redferns 88 (Gene Clarke), 90 (Marvin Gaye); Robert Altman/Retna 89 (Dennis Hopper); Rex Features 70, 78; Time Life/Rex Features 73; James Stafford 120; Virginia Turbett 95; VF Corporation 58, 62; Jean Baptiste-Mondino/WEA 111; Dan Budnik/Woodfin Camp Associates 82 (de Kooning).